A BOOK OF LIFE

MARTIN GRAY

A BOOK OF LIFE TO FIND HAPPINESS, COURAGE & HOPE

A *Continuum Book*
THE SEABURY PRESS/New York

The Seabury Press
815 Second Avenue
New York, N. Y. 10017

Second Printing

Translation copyright © 1975 by The Seabury Press, Inc.
Printed in the United States of America
Editor: Michael Roloff
Designed by S.S. Drate
Original edition: *Le Livre de la Vie* © Éditions Robert Laffont, S.A.,
1973

Library of Congress Cataloging in Publication Data

Gray, Martin.
  A book of life.

  (A Continuum book)
  Translation of Le livre de la vie.
  1.   Gray, Martin. I. Title.
DS135.F9G713   170'.202 [B]   74-14560
ISBN 0-8164-9225-5

3-29-76

To those who by the thousands
have written to tell me their friendship.
To those who silently
have shared my hardship.
To those who have asked
about the meaning of life.
For those and for all
who have, at one time in life,
experienced sadness,
solitude, illness
and despair.
For all those
who have needed a friend's voice
that answers the question
Why?
For all those, these pages
to help them
find in themselves happiness,
courage and hope.

I wish to thank Madame H. O. Erikson with whom I first talked about writing this book. Her remarks helped me to clarify my thoughts. She read the manuscript and made many valuable suggestions.

Contents

Thousands of people from all over the world have written to Martin Gray, who survived the Warsaw Ghetto and Treblinka as a boy and, most recently, the deaths of his wife and children in a forest fire, about his autobiography For Those I Loved. *They have praised his tenacity, his courage, and his enduring faith in man; they have told him how this book gave them the strength to live, and they have asked him to share his wisdom with them. Martin Gray answers these questions in* A BOOK OF LIFE.

THE SKY AND THE WORD

I had never looked at the sky as I had this evening.

I was coming back from the city at close of dusk. I had left the noise and uproar of the road behind me, gone beyond the last houses. Beneath me I saw the lights of the avenues. I had found silence.

There seemed nothing else between the sky and earth.

Arrived on this upland, I had no wish to return to my house, empty as a deserted ship. I walked across the fields toward trees that stood on the horizon like a torn curtain. There was a gentle warmth that evening after the intense heat of the day. The scent of dry plants rose from the earth. I was walking, at peace for the first time in months.

No doubt it was because of the elderly lady who had approached me that afternoon. I was signing my book *For Those I Loved,* and men and women were filing past the little table I sat behind. They shook my hand, I said a few words and signed.

But my mind was elsewhere, full of sounds and images as each time I greeted my readers. For them, who was I? A

man who had survived, who was handing them a book. I
surprised them: "I thought you'd be older," they often said.
Sometimes they began to tell me of their lives. I listened to
them, but there were other voices in me.

Those of my own. I heard the shrieks that rose from the
depths of murdered Europe, where I had lived with death
as a companion. I heard the laughter of my children as they
ran toward me. I saw the ruins of burned out towns, bodies
turned to stone, and I saw the burning forest, my family
whom I looked for in vain.

I signed. I listened but I was elsewhere, with my
memories that did not leave me, that lived in me. At times,
when someone was standing before me, I forgot his presence. My hand hesitated. It was as if I'd been seized with
vertigo.

Where am I? Who is this man sitting in front of an open
book? Is it you? These photographs of those you love, of
yourself as a child, of your children and your wife, why are
they imprisoned in these pages? What book is this? Who are
these people looking at you? What do they want?

And then, I came to.

I signed. These photographs and words were the story
of my life, of my happiness and misery, my struggle and
hope. I was the survivor. I knew that I was right to be there,
to transmit my message. I knew, because thousands of
readers had written to me that my words rang true and had
borne witness in all countries. I had received letters from
Italy and Japan, America and Africa, Germany and Poland,

France and England. From women and men, children and old people, professors and peasants. Each had wanted to express his emotion to me, to thank me. Their letters went to those I loved. I was merely a survivor, a necessary witness. This was what I had survived for.

But I was not at peace. I felt life so tenacious in myself that at times it was too much for me. At times, as those books were handed to me, I felt a temptation to flee, to hide myself. To keep my story for myself alone, to live huddled over my misery.

Nonetheless, I went on signing since I'd made a commitment—in their memory, and because each reader became for me another reason for continuing. They gave me confidence. I owed it to myself to go forward. To be faithful to their image of me. My life was full with theirs.

It was not easy. Until this afternoon, contrary to appearances, anxiety had been my cancer. I smiled at others. In myself I was crying.

And then this old woman had come up to me.

She held herself straight against the table with my book to her chest. She was smiling. And behind her smile I seemed to see other old faces; that of my mother welcoming me after I'd reached America with such difficulty. Those of other women glimpsed amid ruins in Warsaw, seen an instant and then lost forever. The old woman began to gently speak to me.

"Your book," she said, "has saved a life." She told me how her daughter had been desperate, unable to go on enduring a life in which her dreams were shattered one after the other.

"Her life has been hard—it's true," the old woman said.

By chance she came across my book, my life, of those I loved. And something happened.

"I can't explain it to you," her mother told me. "She is not the same. She can live now, she has found work. I truly think she will come through." She held her book tightly to her chest.

"Would you like me to sign your book?" I asked. I had to say something.

She shook her head.

"I didn't come for that," she answered. "I wanted to thank you."

She put her hand on my shoulder.

"You must continue, continue to speak, to tell people. They do not know. Sometimes a few words are enough. How, one doesn't know, but they are and everything changes for them. It's as if they'd suddenly discovered what they had not seen."

She was gone.

I continued to sign. But her phrases resonated in my mind. And others came back to me, phrases that I'd read too quickly, that had recurred in all the letters and that had given me strength to live even while disquieting me. Now, because of this old woman's face which reminded me of so many others, all these phrases came to life in me. I understood.

Words and the Word are an unsuspected force. They are torment or a soothing breeze. The rain that devastates or the water that irrigates.

I had already learned that there are words that kill. Those of orders barked out by officers in black uniforms, and thousands left for the trenches; others that sufficed to transform men, innocent until then, into executioners, and others that made the innocent guilty.

I knew also that there were words of tenderness and hope, words of happiness which are the sun of a life.

But to know is nothing; what you know must become your blood.

That old woman had suddenly made me understand that words are infinitely powerful when they are not merely an arrangement of letters but the flesh of a life.

If the words of *For Those I Loved* had had so much power, the power to change a life, it was because I had written them with my sorrow, my hope, my will; they were the voice of those I had loved, those to whom I had given my face, my name.

I left the bookstore in peace for the first time in years, since the fire had devastated my life.

There are encounters that modify the colors of things. That make blaze out what had been underground.

My words, my word had found the road of that young
woman who until then had refused to hope. The words of
her mother had entered me and given me peace. Strength
and authority of words when they are true.

But who still speaks?
Who dares to ask the questions that each carries in him-
self?

We are taken in the iron circle of our habits, of our pro-
fessional constraints. What we live by and speak of are our
vocations, our desires and pleasures.

And yet, one day, because such is life, we are thunder-
struck by fate or encounter misfortune. And we always will,
for those we love are condemned to disappear. Then, because we have never dared speak of that which truly counts,
we lose our footing. We fall into anguish, we no longer
know how to face the world.

I have been immersed in hell since my childhood. I
knew that life was no easy road, that men were mortal, and I
also knew that at the heart of happiness may surge up the
dreaded misery. But I knew that happiness was real, that
one may create it, and that hope was not merely an illusion.

This evening, walking in fields whose earth was still
warm with the sun, I felt a peace within me like strength,
and as I approached the trees I saw my life again, step by
step.

I had known barbarism, men who were evil; I had
known the sacrifice of men who were good. I had known
cities at war and the war men make in cities at peace. Then

love, children running here in the fields in which I was walking. And fire, that inferno that had destroyed my life for the second time. I had told the story of all this. For myself and for those I loved.

And my voice had spoken to others.

And others had helped me. First of all my people, for I am a Jew. Of course my family had belonged to the re-formed religion, and before the war I had not clearly known what it meant to be a Jew. Then the Nazis entered Warsaw. They had made me wear an armband and a star of David. They killed my people. It was they who made me realize that I was a Jew and I acquired the will to be one. I remember that officer who struck me in a prison cell. I thought I would die there on the floor under his blows when I felt myself, apparently defeated, much stronger than he. Victorious. I belonged to a community, a people whom history had often hunted, whom emperors and kings had often wished to destroy. And yet this community had survived. And I would survive.

We were not superior to others but, perhaps because we had been persecuted and had known how to preserve our faith, we had become more obstinate, more resistant, more determined to follow our life through.

I had cried to that officer, "I am a Jew and you will not kill me. You will never kill me." I was proud. If animals with the faces of men struck us, if executioners martyred us, it was because we did not belong to the same race as they. Thank God.

Since then I had learned better what it is to belong to

the Jewish people. It seems to me that my life, my modest
life, parallels that of my people. It is reborn from attempts
to destroy it. From the inferno of war Israel surged into
existence. Like my people, I will never renounce life.

I came near the trees.

I sat down on the ground. I spread my arms, palms out-
ward to the sky.

Never had I looked at this infinite sea, bluish and bril-
liant, as I did this evening.

Never.

In the forests of Europe during the war I had studied the
sky for signs of the snow that would cover my traces, or for
the sun that would dry my body. In the loud cities I had
forgotten the sky, it was nothing more than the pink and
yellow reflection of glimmering flags.

Later, here, I had considered the sky only as the kingdom of light, intense and joyous, alive.

Sometimes, on nights like this one, we would go up onto
the terrace. Holding my arm, my children held their fingers
up to the Great Bear, and looked for the Milky Way. They
cried out at the sight of a falling star.

I looked for them tonight, those dying stars that disappeared after brilliantly flashing out. They pass, and the universe is as it was, one star the less. Nothing. And infinity.

A star is like a life that's effaced in mankind's billions.
And each star, each man is a universe. When it dies all
dies, and all goes on.

Never had I looked at the sky as I did that evening.

For years, during my three lives—that of embattled violence, that of the struggle to succeed and that of absolute happiness—I had never had the time or the courage to look at the sky. And I understood why men do not look at it. They bury themselves in acts, in war and in joys. As I had buried myself. They forget this sky that envelops the world, this sky that is the same for all. They wish to forget it as I had forgotten it. And the cities with their tall buildings, their gray smoke and lights, dissimulate it. One no longer has to flee it. It no longer exists.

This sky I was looking at.

My gaze lost itself in the Milky Way. I followed the trajectory of a star, and I understood.

I had refused to look at the sky. I had fled those white trails across a dark ocean, those millions of coagulated stars, fled that question that arises in us when we look at the sky, *Why?* I had fled it and yet behind me were three extreme lives implicit with this question. My father, my sons, my wife, my mother—I had seen them perish. And thousands of others.

I had seen my happiness surge up in an instant and disappear at once, like a mirage.

I had seen Evil and Good.

The beast with a man's face that kills, and the man who begs alms and gives his life.

But who could say that any, even the man of a gentle, peaceful life, the man who was sleeping at this moment by his wife's side in this town by the sea, had not encountered this *Why?* That he would not see the angry axe of fate come down on his own?

I was lying on the ground, in the silence.

A faint breath of air rose from the valley. I remained immobile, alone, as if I were the first or the last man to look at this sky under which so many lives had passed, so many to come, to begin, to finish, to suffer. So many lives which like my own refused to see the sky because it would have meant facing the question *Why?*

And the other questions which sprang from this word.

> *Why the sky, why man, why me, why life, why death, why executioners and victims, why happiness and misery?*
>
> *And beyond that, what is there? Is it chance, destiny, a god of justice or simply the unknown that escapes our questions?*

Why?

That word in the sky above me. That word which I could no longer evade, that I ought not to flee since it imposed itself on me, because of that old woman that afternoon, and her daughter who had drawn strength from my words.

Perhaps if I answered those questions aloud someone would hear, would find in my questions the strength to look at the sky. Perhaps my words would help them.

Once, to the city ringed by the executioners, I had brought wheat and this was my profit, my joy, my risk and my help to others.

I could still make another trip, break through a new wall, the wall which enclosed each man and locked him in himself. I could bring something, not a sack of grain this time, but my experience and the lessons I'd drawn from it.

I had been defeated so many times and conquered defeat so many times that perhaps my voice would be heard.

It was no longer a question of telling my life, but simply of questioning myself. To try to understand, to tell what I had learned, in a Book of Life.

I got up, leaving the earth, and I walked in the forest among the burned trees of which some were returning to life. Shoots were coming up among the blackened bark. There where all had seemed lost, no doubt in a few years a true forest would be reborn. Birds would come back to it.

I was walking.

The town was far away, down by the sea. A light mist covered it, blurring the lights and muffling sounds. And preventing men from looking at the sky and asking the questions of their life. Questions which they would have to ask.

Those who, like myself, sought to know what they were and what they should be.

Those who, like myself, might one day find themselves alone, in the solitude of stones thrown down in a field.

Those who—and I had known this hope—awaited love. Perhaps they were living it.

Those who had known death, when the tree which they had thought eternal had suddenly split and fallen.

13

Those who, like myself, had given—or would give—life, marvelling at seeing the spring grow and become a river. Those who perhaps had seen it dry up. Those who wished for happiness, who feared the law of destiny.

Those who lived without knowing and who, sometimes as in a flash of lightning that blinded them, questioned themselves, perceived the immense sky and shuddered in asking themselves why.

I went into my house. I did not turn the lights on. I remained in darkness, in night. I still saw the sky, and through the bay window the vague glow that rose from the town.

I was at peace.

Before me was a task. Before me words which I had to assemble, order, speak. Words, the answers to these questions, my questions. Words which perhaps would serve for others.

Because the same sky envelops us. Because we are made of the same elements.

Because we are all men.

And because the word, when it is true, can help, like a brother's hand.

THE
SOURCE

W*hat am I that all this has happened to me?*

Each morning, when I awake, this question torments me.

I look at myself in the mirror. Is it possible that this history belongs to me? Is it I who have come out of hell, who have known happiness, have seen life destroyed and now find myself alone, a survivor?

Is it I?

I look at myself. Who am I then? It seems to me that I have hardly changed. I recognize in my face, slightly more wrinkled, the features of the child I was, of the young man armed and on the run, and those of my son. And yet this history was mine. It was in me, I had lived it.

Who am I then? Why has all this happened to me?

I walk out into the clear light of morning, but I feel a thick darkness within me. I am a mystery to myself. I do not understand.

I walk. Beyond the trees lives a solitary peasant. He
does not work much. Only enough to support himself. He
has but one passion: to paint. He paints on scraps of cardboard, on burlap which he primes and then dries in the sun.
No one has ever taught him to draw. When he was eight he
was already working in the fields.

This morning, I come across him sitting on a rock by the
road, a board across his knees. His eyes are half-closed because he is looking at the sun. He scarcely turns his head
when he sees me. I stop by him.

"I want to get the color of dawn, you understand? Light
is constantly changing."

I remain still, observing.

"Why do you paint? You. . . ."

He shrugs his shoulders, interrupting me.

"It's that way, it's in me, always has been. I have the
need in myself."

In myself also I have felt these needs that one cannot
repress, that reason and wise caution cannot restrain. A
need to fight, to return to the city in ruins, a need to survive
and conquer, and today the need to continue so as to express, to comprehend a need like that of the peasant's.

This need is the heart of ourselves.
Our burning heart. Mysterious. Which makes us what
we are.
But who put this force in us?
Who opens up weakness in us?
We can be saved by one, but lost by the other.

Further down the road, toward the town, there is a white house. I know it well. My family and I stopped there often. My children loved to climb the trees that bordered the garden. We would chat with the old couple that lived there. A man with a furrowed, smiling face, with an inner gaiety, taking my children in his arms and lifting them to the first branches. A silent man whose eyes spoke. His wife, plump, her hands folded on her knees, unlike him talkative but with sad eyes and melancholy voice, constantly talking of her youth, the past, the happy times she had known so long ago that perhaps they existed only in her memories. Her memories were a wound that devoured her. Two persons who had lived side by side the same life, from which one had emerged serene, joyous and calm, the other buried in the shifting sands of yearning for days gone forever.

Why these differences between one person and another? Where did some draw their strength from, and where did others find their taste for sadness and resignation?

In my adolescence, when I faced war and the hell made by men, I had already learned to recognize, just by their look, those who would fight and those who would give up, let death take them.

This morning, I passed by the white house. The man was in the garden, under a tree. He waved to me.

"What beautiful weather we're having," he said. "Unbelievable this year. Beautiful, not too hot."

His face was smiling.

"And your wife?"

"She's still asleep," he said. "She can't sleep nights, she lies awake for hours and then takes something toward morning. So she stays in bed. Too bad, she's missing the morning sunlight."

There were millions who missed the morning sunlight, millions whose thoughts, like nibbling insects, prevented them from finding sleep. Millions who tried to silence their heads by taking pills each night.

Wasn't this giving up?

When I experienced absolute misery, that unforeseeable torment in which my loved ones vanished, a doctor wanted to immerse me a long while in unconsciousness.

"You will wake up later, time will have passed," he told me. "This cure will save you."

I refused it. I had experienced nights of madness, pounding my head against the ground, clutching what remained of my loved ones, the few playthings of my children. I had cried out. But I was here now, having gotten through those nights, having suffered but with open eyes. Not having fled it.

"Not everyone has your strength," the doctor told me. "There are some who must forget."

My strength? At times I felt myself so weak, so fragile, so close to succumbing. But I did not want to disappear. That was my only strength. A resolution directed not to the past but to the future.

I did not wish to forget, but I did not wish to shroud myself in memories.

"But you are strong, exceptionally so," the doctor concluded, shaking his head.

I had nothing to convince him of, but I knew that I was no stronger than others. I had seen old women exhausted from hunger and paralyzed by fear, suddenly recover because they wanted to save a loved one. I had seen them run, fight, conquer.

> *For each man, each woman can find in themselves the strength.*
> *There is a powerful spring in us. An energy stronger than a thousand suns.*
> *But who knows this spring?*
> *It is hidden by evil weeds that stifle it.*
> *And we are deaf to its murmuring.*
> *At times it comes to animate certain of our acts, then we leave it, sometimes to die.*

I had been forced to discover it. Otherwise I could not live. I had channelled it, and it had borne me, thrust me ahead and I am still in its current.

But others?

This woman in her white house who regretted the years gone by, endlessly looking back on them, what had she done with her source? Had it dried up? Worse perhaps. She was flowing backward, a raging current insidiously sapping where it should irrigate and transport. I had seen that also. Men who had become executioners of others. That friend who wanted to turn me in and those I loved in hope of saving himself. People who for a piece of bread were willing to become the servants of death, lackeys of the men in black uniforms.

The source in them was no more than a muddy, troubled water. It battered them, blinded them and soon submerged them.

I remember Paul. It was no longer the war but he also had allowed his source to be polluted.

He envied me. He tried indirectly to find out what my projects were so he could outdo them, gain on me, quickly succeed at my expense. I let him do it. Why tire myself competing with him when the vast field of all that was possible opened before me?

I saw Paul again recently. Aged, bitter, he'd become his own executioner. His source had slowly destroyed him because he had directed it at others and, in the end, against himself.

For there can be no boundary between one's self and the others. He who thinks that his self is the unique center of the world, who refuses to see that he is one among all men, will one day know extreme misery and barrenness.

I have so often seen this, in men walled up in their pride, jealously protecting their possessions, trying to let nothing escape of what they imagine to be their eternal riches. They have realized the power of the source in themselves but have wanted to use it as a weapon against others, or simply as their own property.

In a time of hunger, in a world of horror, I knew a strong man who had what was then the supreme fortune: bread. He had abandoned his family because he knew that he could only eat if he lived alone. He never went out. Immured in himself as in a fort he was afraid, waiting for a knock on the door. And one day they searched the building and found him, pushed him outside and marched him off to his death. He was near me in the column. I was just a boy but I knew where we were going. He knew nothing but his own egotism. He had lived huddled in himself, blinded, forgetting that around him a city was being depopulated. Suddenly he found himself empty, dispossessed of what had been his strength: his goods, his hoarded bread. It was his very greed and isolation that undid him. He had nothing but himself.

Man is nothing when his heart is empty.

This man broke under the first blows like a hollow statue.

No doubt it was then, in hardship, that I learned to see men for what they are.

*We must not allow ourselves to be distracted by the
words, the appearances, functions or honors behind
which men hide.*
*A man's truth is in himself. That is his riches. That is his
true strength.*

I had walked back up to the plateau toward my house.
The sun was now high above the horizon. The peasant had
left his stone by the roadside. I saw him bent over in his
garden, his cap pushed back on his head, whistling. He was
gaiety itself. Often in the evening someone would come
from the village to look for him, simply to have him at their
table, to play cards with him or to hear him talk. Because he
spoke well and because, above all, the breath of happiness
entered with him.

His whistling accompanied me as I walked home. This
joy, this source that radiated from the peasant, where did it
come from if not from the harmony of the man's heart? He
had wanted to paint, he'd been borne forward by this desire
to its fulfillment. He didn't erect barriers between this desire and its completion. He had known how to strip himself,
to accept necessary sacrifices.

Sometimes in winter I would see that no smoke was
coming from his chimney.

I went to see him. "You have no fire in this weather?"

He was in a corner of his room by the window, priming
cardboard surfaces and canvases, his head wrapped in a
thick scarf.

"I don't have the time to spare from painting."

He did not have enough money to buy wood and did not wish to spend his time gathering it. But the heat of his passion warmed his fingers. That was it. It was his source utilized that gave him his gaiety. And as the countryman had made the joy of living blossom in himself, it went well for him with others. Often in winter the villagers would bring him wood.

"Here, you old fool," they'd say. "Warm up or you'll freeze."

He'd laugh at this, and quickly sketching the head of his visitor, hand him the picture.

"Thank you, thank you. Keep this as a souvenir," he'd say.

To be at peace with others you must be at peace with yourself; there must flow in us, freely and joyously, that source which is at the origin of our being, our personality.

After the war, when I'd determined to become rich, when I made money in ever-increasing amounts, a moment came when I no longer knew why I was working for it. I had succeeded, but I who had wanted to find a woman with whom I'd create life was still alone. I had lost hope of finding such a woman.

The source which had borne me thus far now reversed its current, against me and against others.

This was the time I felt myself become savage, tempted to wipe out my competitors. I experienced the double-faced envy of wanting to destroy others and myself. Then I met the woman who was to become my wife, Dina. A flash of lightning and in myself, peace. Once more the stream flowed toward others. I felt myself inundated with joy. I was my old generous self.

> *To realize what you have need of, to let your deeper self be born which so often we stifle, to go toward yourself, toward that springing source in the heart of man—that is the first step toward others. For too often we are a stranger to ourselves. It is that other person in us, the true self, that we must make welcome.*

Thus for a long time I thought I was a businessman; and so I was in the census, I bought and I sold.

Then, when I settled in this house on its plateau, when my children were born, when I had ploughed the land with them, planted the first fruit trees, I knew that I had, only then, achieved my truth. To be a father, to give life, to see my sons and daughters grow up with these trees that nourish man.

I was no longer a stranger to myself. That peasant, my neighbor, who paints untiringly is no longer a stranger to his true self. That is what gives him peace.

> *To discover our source, to find the direction of the current that bears us, to become what we should be, to*

recognize and accept ourselves, to bring to the light
that self which is in us–that is to take on the face of a
man. That is when cruel, concealed hate will end.
Freed from regret and rancor, there is no more hatred
of self. Then you will be able to recognize and accept
the world and others for what they are.
Then, man is a man.

But the road is long.

For years, when I was trapped in the furnace of war, when I too wore a uniform, when I shared with millions of others the duty to kill, I learned that hatred is like raw whiskey. It warms, it gives courage and blinds to danger, it helps one to kill and to die.

Perhaps I myself succumbed to its intoxication for days and months.

Sorrow was too strong in me, the need for revenge too great. I gave in to it, but unwillingly. In my heart, I felt disgust for myself.

I tried to partake of this hatred which buoyed us all, but renascent disgust in the forest at night kept me from sleeping.

Where would be our victory if we became like our enemies?

One evening, after a skirmish in the ruins of a village, we took a prisoner back to the forest. I still see his anxious face now, covered with black sweaty dust, his hair matted, his lips trembling. We had to make him talk. He was bound to a tree. We looked at him laughingly. It was a laughter that made my throat and skin burn red.

"What do you want to know? I'll tell you everything," he said.

His eyes were wild as he looked from one face to another searchingly. I drew back under the trees. My hatred had suddenly died, like plunging your face into a bucket of cold water after drinking too much.

I returned to the group.

The man was talking. He was giving the positions and intentions of the soldiers, his comrades, who encircled us. Fear and humiliation had unmanned him.

"We don't have to kill him," I said.

The others shrugged their shoulders. We had to attack soon to escape. The man was killed. But I no longer hated.

I remember the faces of so many men and women whom I encountered briefly, for a glance, in the camps of hell. There where a life mattered less than a crust of bread. I also knew, in our city, men who revolted me.

All those thin-faced men, heads slightly bowed, who refused to fight for their lives, who refused to hate. They went to their deaths calmly, tranquilly.

I had chosen another way: combat. And we were right to resist. I know we were. But I learned not to condemn those righteous men. I understand them better today than I could then.

They were what remained to us of goodness.

They testified that man, no matter what the circumstances, can refuse to kill and to hate. With their martyred bodies, they defended us against hate. They remained true to their faith. To themselves.

We could not, we should not, have followed their example. The time had not yet come for it.

But because they were steadfast as the rocks, they saved us. I saw them again, herded by the black-uniformed soldiers among the standing walls of our ruined city, saying to the soldiers:

"I die without hatred for you."

In the eyes of these men, battered by blows on their way to death, there was pity for their executioners.

At that time I stood against them. "Revolt, fight!" I would have cried to them. I was right, and I was wrong. For their way of accepting death, defying barbarism by submission to its laws, was also a revolt. They fought with their eyes and their pity. Without them by our sides, what would we have been if not like our enemies?

Ours was the just fight because these men had died without hatred.

They were, without our knowing it—and even though I'd cursed them—the proof that we were on the right way.

And their example would, in some of us, bear fruit one day.

For he who shows himself to others with the sole force of his self, he who is true, who speaks without artifice and who refuses hatred, the just man who is in har-

*mony with himself, whatever his personal fate–he is
heard by others.*
And his source does not die. It springs anew elsewhere.

Often I would see two or three strollers or farmhands on
their way back to the village pause behind my friend the
peasant.

"So, you're going on with it," one would say. "I hope
you're selling some."

To sell.

To sell, that is the thing. I have been selling for years. I
have accumulated money and goods. And I was poor in
myself. Of course, it is hard not to have money. But the true
misery is that of the desperate man. Poverty may give rise to
despair. But success does not dispel it.

"Sell my paintings? I should pay for the privilege of
painting."

My neighbor the peasant turned around and pointed his
brush at the farmhand.

"I am the rich one. Painting is my luxury. Do you know
that? I paint what I want and when I want, and I know what
gives me pleasure. I am doing what I was born to do."

And he began to paint, whistling. The others said nothing, suddenly grave and hesitant, studying this man in his
blue cloth jacket which the sun had nearly bleached. Per-
ceiving as they looked that he had found peace, the way to

be himself. That he had listened to the inner voice, heard the source, and allowed it to flourish.

They looked at him and at themselves in him. Questioning themselves.

Everyone knows that there is within him a voice that speaks, a simple, clear voice that too often he stifles. For it is a demanding voice, strict as a straight line.
This voice, this source that we silence speaks the truth, gives the means to achieve the equilibrium and liberation of the self.
But we are afraid to be ourselves.

We are afraid to liberate this source, to let it jet free. Everything conspires to make us deaf to this voice. Prudence and apparent reason.

In our city, shut up in its walls guarded by men ready to kill, when death prowled at the gates, when our executioners promised us a slave's life, but a life, if we would submit quietly to them, only a few were willing to look within themselves, to hear that mad voice which said, "One must remain free, man must be free, you must not submit to the laws of these animals with men's faces."

It would have been easier to be lulled into security with the others, to accept, to believe our executioners, to wait, penned in our ghetto like vanquished animals.

Some of us refused submission, the false shows of reason. The young, especially those in whom the source still ran strong and lively, had learned to listen attentively to the inner voice of their being, to respect the prime necessities.

> *A man does not submit to the unacceptable.*
> *A man respects in himself the jewel which is his being as*
>   *a man. He refuses to let it be disgraced.*
> *Whatever the price that must be paid.*

Those who choose to follow the narrow, dangerous way ordained for them by their being often die for it.

Jacob was my age. We often met in the courtyard of a building. The violence of war surrounded us. Everyone in his family refused to see what was coming. Everyone accepted the fate marked out for them by the executioners. They all sought to hush their inner voice, because it said that to resist was the true wisdom now. That death would be the reward of cowardice.

One day, when the worst of winter was past, Jacob came to see me. He knew that I was regularly crossing the enemy barricades.

"Help me to get through," he said.

"You know the risks?"

"I can't stay here any longer. I can't look at it, can't accept it. I can't stand it any longer."

He repeated these words of refusal, strong words born of his whole being. "Okay. Come tomorrow."

Luck was not with us. Additional sentries had been

stationed, which I knew nothing about. I managed to get away. Jacob was caught. He must have died that same day.

He stayed with me a long time in memory, that comrade of the thin face and blond hair. I long regretted having guided him to a liberty which took the guise of death. A few weeks later, the executioners began to empty the city of its inhabitants, leading them out to death.

All the prudent ones, those who had obeyed the law and dried up the source of their personality, all perished.

The true prudence is to hear in yourself the voice of refusal, to respect the man in yourself.

If thousands, hundreds of thousands of us who were shut in by the walls of hunger, fear and humiliation had given this will free play, the men in black uniforms, the executioners, would have been disarmed and defeated.

Today, there is peace.

But it is always as difficult for us to be ourselves. This is because, although the war has ended, *it always requires courage to be your true self, to construct your life in harmony with the demands of that voice which is in us and which is us.*

There are so many chances to nobly resign ourselves. How often are we tempted to be like others for the sake of a false peace, by the repression of one's self!

When I arrived in that new country, the United States, in complete ignorance of its language, customs and laws, I had to quickly find a way to make my living. I was offered quiet jobs, sure jobs. I had only to accept them to have a smooth road ahead of me. I refused. I don't regret having done so, no matter what troubles I had. I was faithful to myself. To the irrepressible source that I felt well up within me, that I did not know and neither wished nor was able to contain. I fled the advice of good sense.

"It's a miracle that you already have what you do. What more do you want?"

My uncle was a peaceful, gentle man. He shook his head, puzzled by my obstinacy in looking for something else. He thought me unstable, and explained my refusals by my youth, my lack of experience.

"You don't know, it's difficult here. Keep what you have."

I laughed. He thought my motive was gain, the foolish ambition for money. It was true that I wished to escape poverty. But that was not the key to my attitude: my ambition was greater than he thought. I wished to be myself. And I knew that I would have to go on struggling, choose uncertainty rather than settling down. And I was confident. Suffering, enemies, war and hunger and misery had been my teachers. I had learned to know myself, discover myself.

Death and violence had entered my life when I was barely an adolescent. The executioners had so often thrust me against a wall, covering me with their guns, shouting "Who are you?" that I had been forced to accept myself: as a Jew, as a man.

My enemies and executioners, I can thank you for your lessons.

When I saw one of them, lips clenched in the pleasure of killing, attack one of us, when I saw them tear a baby away from its mother and fight among themselves for stolen gold, *I knew then that there is an animal in man and that life consists in not letting it dominate you.*

I lived in fear of letting this animal rule in me, disguising itself in my appearance, taking my face.

Often I felt it stir in me, leave its lair, direct my acts.

When I entered a conquered enemy town I would laugh as I made the inhabitants humiliate themselves. Later, when I got the better of a rival I was tempted to make him surrender so that my victory would be complete.

This animal that prowled in my inner darkness—my executioners had taught me to be wary of it. To tame it. I had seen what happened to the man who let himself be led by it. At first, it is content with little. Then, like a tiger enraged by the sight of prey, it roars and maddens itself. The man is no longer in control. He is no more than an instrument, a sum total of appetites and passions. An animal with a man's face.

If there is war, he is an executioner or a coward. He kills or he flees. If there is peace, he is like a man at war. Pitiless.

I knew a dealer on New York City's Third Avenue who held his suppliers by the throat. Nothing could soften him.

"You think I'm hard in business," he said to me. "Isn't that so?"

He laughed and rubbed his hands.

"It's the law of the jungle. Business is like the jungle—it's either eat or be eaten. I prefer to be the lion."

He was not the lion. He was barely a hyena, scenting from afar the prey, starved yet afraid, ready to run for it. A grizzled beast who found its only glory with the weakest, the victims. Darkness had won out in him. In him the animal had become master.

> *And the danger is in each man. For each man has an animal's violence in himself. Defeat awaits us at each moment.*
> *We retain our face, our appearances, but within us the man may become a slave and the darkness efface us.*
> *In the depths of our forest a black monster has risen up. He has captured the source and wallows in it.*

But only a few are aware of this menace. I grew up in the kingdom of victorious evil.

I was the witness of its triumph.

That neighbor of ours, a dignified and quiet man who always doffed his hat courteously to us and who one day, when my father was being hunted, came to our house, shoved my mother aside and took several precious objects for himself.

"These are mine now," he said to me grimacing. "You're done for."

I had seen, in the queues that formed by fountains or the

river for water, men and women kick at other men and women in a sudden rage, stone them, shouting "Death to Jews!" And I had seen us reduced to the status of a herd, and the blank gaze of the executioners.

I knew the existence of the animal in man. I identified in myself the demands of this masked force, powerful and ready to spring. The unconscious, perhaps. Those demons that civilization holds pent up in us, that sometimes break their chains, or often learn to disguise themselves and live among us with men's faces. The unconscious. History, the whole history of violence, of the animal, and original man-animal.

A few days were enough to show me *how frail those facades are behind which men hide their demons.* A few days of hunger, a few days of fear, and men were fighting and killing each other on a street corner near a pile of garbage in which they hoped to find something edible. I saw men betray each other for a loaf of bread, cutting each other's throats for a plate of soup. I saw skeleton-like children dying in the streets of frost, while fat men indifferently passed by. On the wall that enclosed us, the Germans amused themselves by taking potshots at children out scavenging for a few potatoes. And whenever they hit one, passersby would laugh and applaud the murder.

I saw it.

Barbarism, the savage unconscious, can prevail in us. Because in each of us there exists the long, the living,

*the many times ten-thousand-year history–barbaric,
savage, animal–of man. Because each time a human
being comes into the world the whole human past is
reborn. A past which he is ignorant of and may therefore succumb beneath its weight.*

Nevertheless, when I saw my children run toward me,
when they laughingly dragged me toward the cherry tree
and made me lift them to the branches heavy with fruit, I
forgot that violent element in them as in all of us, that
dangerous possibility that I would have to teach them to see
in themselves, to master.

I went home with them; they hid behind the cypresses
along the road, ran down the aisles of peach trees. I lost
sight of them. I heard their cries. Their mother appeared in
the doorway, called them to her with a wave of her hand
and they came running. I saw them again, scuffling on the
grass, half-naked in the setting sun.

And one evening, suddenly, perhaps because of their
running, I remembered other figures running, of pitiably
thin children who fled silently down a street. I was
stretched prone, my head scarcely raised above a window-
sill on the first floor; I saw the soldier aiming his gun at
them. He was bareheaded, his blond hair bright in the sunlight, and laughing. As young as I was then, almost a boy in
his black uniform too big for him. One of the children,
targets bearing the star of David, fell to the pavement. The
soldier turned to his comrades, shouting for joy.

"I got one!" he shouted. "I got one!" He laughed like a boy at the shooting gallery of a fair.

What had happened to this boy to make him a killer?

Later, I entered his country as a victor. I saw other children, as thin as those he had fired on, children crouched by the carcasses of horses, children clumsily filling tins with the stagnant water of ponds. They were defenseless, innocent. Like my children. And yet it had been possible to turn them into killers like those young soldiers.

Childhood is a spring of water that irrigates the man to come. It can drown him.

With this water of origin, man can make his way through life. He can quench his thirst or poison himself with it.

One must be careful with childhood.

I was careful with my own children. The destiny or the chance, which I must call destiny, or the forces—perhaps the Force—that decides the lot of men, saw fit to deprive me of them, did not allow me to see what they would have become. And I am alone.

But I did my utmost to defend them from themselves. We were always there, Dina and myself, to alert them to the world. Nicole, Suzanne, Charles, Richard. Because I knew that life is terribly brief.

I wished for my children, when they opened their eyes on the world, to see their mother and father at their side, like two strong trees who would protect them from storms.

To have my time free, to devote it to them, I decided to give up business. What was money worth?

Nothing is more important for a man than to guide another's life.

I did not want to fail in this task.

It was for that reason that we left the city, a world which contained our friends and pleasures. It was not our wish to simplify ourselves in isolation, but simply to devote ourselves to our children.

For both of us had seen too many children grow up like weeds at the mercy of the streets and hazard.

I will always remember Betty. Both of her parents were workers of modest circumstances. I often met them in the doorway of the building where my grandmother lived. Their lives were hurried, time-ridden. The mother overly made up, hiding her fatigue under rouge and powder, masking her fear of age in flashy clothes. The husband walking in front with lowered head, and Betty skipping behind them, finishing buttoning her coat, eyes half closed, still heavy with sleep. Her mother would turn around and say:

"Hurry up! Hurry up!"

That was the phrase I heard every time.

Betty followed them. Where was she going? To school or a baby-sitter? I saw Betty grow up. Without a childhood.

She already had the grey skin of the passersby, too rapidly aged by the city and disappointments.

Then my grandmother died. I no longer visited the building. Years later, during one of my trips to New York, I met Betty's father by chance. I was in a hurry, anxious to return to my family, to finish what I had come for and leave the city. I apologized for having bumped into him and picked up his hat.

"I know you," he said.

I tried to remember, annoyed at losing time.

"I know you, do you remember. . .?"

"Betty," I said simply.

He took my hand. "Yes, Betty. I have to tell you."

He clung to me, telling me the story of his life since then, a banal bankruptcy. His daughter Betty had vanished in the city one evening and had not been heard of since.

"It's the times," he said. "What can we do? We did everything for her. You know how she had everything she wanted. Her mother and I worked to bring her up."

I tried to console him. I missed my last appointment. I had to go back. I had to be with my sons and daughters. Too bad if I had no time to buy them presents, so great was my hurry.

The child's first need is not things. It is the company of others. A need to feel at all times the protective shadow, benevolent, attentive, of those who brought him into the world, wished for him.

To give to an infant is to give yourself. At every mo-
ment. Then he may grow up straight, with strong deep
roots.

Mine were that way.

If I had come through so many dangers, and most of all
discouragement and fear; if in the night of our barracks at
the heart of that inferno created by war I had refused to die;
if I had always known while living under the menace of the
men with animals' faces that happiness existed, that in man
there is the possible good—I owed it all to my mother and
father.

Parents are the seed of the child and the earth in which
he grows.
For him, they are the world, the image of what he is,
what he should be or not be. What they do, what they
say, what they are, remain in him. Even if he does not
know it. For the child is always present in the adult.

My mother was the gentleness, the silence which is
wealth. She had no need to speak, for all her acts were full
of love. She reached her hand to my face, and before it
touched my cheek I felt its warmth in myself; I was enveloped by her. Nothing separated us. I was her, and she
was me. When I entered the first enemy towns, ready to
revenge myself on the vanquished killers, it was my

mother's image that held my hand. I remember that town, apparently deserted, that we entered as victors. White linens were hung in the windows as a sign of surrender. We were at war, we had come through destroyed towns, our towns; I still saw the martyred bodies heaped by the thousands in pits. I heard the screams of women and children, and I saw my gray-haired mother disappearing in the herd of victims being driven to its death because they were Jews, my people.

With the other victorious soldiers, I kicked in the doors of the town's squat houses and shouted at the inhabitants to come out of their hiding places.

One after the other they came out of the cellars, hands raised high over their heads, humble, trembling. They were either old or children. As I saw them appear, eyes lowered, the children sometimes daring to steal a look at us, my anger died, my conqueror's laugh, insolent, assured, caught in my throat.

Who were they, these inhabitants who we were forcing to abase themselves? People as poor as we had been, as hundreds of thousands of us had been, conquered people whom defeat had almost rendered innocent, old people who had perhaps approved but above all who had endured, let themselves be swept along.

A child turned back toward the door of a cellar, his face covered with tears. He wiped his nose with the back of his hand. He was waiting for someone to appear. An old woman came out, bent double by age—no doubt his grandmother. Reaching her hand to him she drew him to her, caressing his face as he buried himself in her black pleated skirt.

This hand on a child's cheek; it was my mother with me.

I shouted out an order. My comrades looked at me, shrugging their shoulders and spitting toward the inhabitants as they moved off.

I was the last to leave, turning around to see this old woman and child, one against the other.

My dead mother had saved me from the violent part of myself. Her gentleness and her goodness had prevented me from letting it prevail over me.

What one gives to a child will one day be repaid.
What you refuse to him, he will refuse to you.
And the harm one does to him, he may repeat.
But if one fills his young sails with the wind of strength,
    of courage and of uprightness, then he will skillfully
    navigate the storms of life.

My father gave me strength.

First because I admired him. He had escaped from his prisoner's camp, and was in hiding in the occupied city. I met him far from our house in some square or garden. We walked side by side; I raised my eyes to his and he smiled at me, speaking in a grave, deep voice.

"One must never give in, Martin. That is why I escaped.

Always take the first chance that comes, for there may not be another."

It was not merely what he said: I knew what he had done. I saw him alive.

The true lessons, those that the child hears, those that shape his personality, are the acts of the adult.
To educate a child is to offer him yourself as an example.

"You must keep your pride," my father said, "and that will not be easy."

We separated without embracing, like two men, two equals. He simply placed his hand on my shoulder.

"Be careful. You know that you must not surrender. But be careful."

I have not surrendered.

And when so many years later, at the end of a life which itself was ravaged by misery and conflagration, I found myself alone, it was my father to whom I appealed to defend me from the destruction that was growing more powerful in myself. Despite his death, my father still spoke to me.

He had never hidden from me the suffering and danger that are part of life. Nor the necessary resolve to continue despite them.

One does not protect another, a child or a man, by dis-

*simulating the risks of life, the element of misery that
it contains. To protect someone is first of all to make
him see, to show him the danger within and without
himself. It is to enable him to confront and overcome
it.*

I wanted to be for my children what my father had been
for me.

I observed them, and took account of their differences:
Nicole, sure of herself; Suzanne, sensitive; Charles, active;
and Richard, whose gaiety I already perceived.

But it is not easy to be a parent.

When I had to decide between two courses of action,
severity or indulgence, caution or risk, I would say to myself, thinking of my father, "What would he have done?"

I tried to remember comparable situations. To relive in
myself confrontations which we'd had. When he locked me
in my room to keep me from braving the enemy barricades
every day, when I managed to get out and when finally he
had let me go on risking my life.

Fortunately, it was peacetime now. But when Charles
wanted to climb the trees alone, when Nicole ran toward
the rocky cove where the sea raged and foamed, I had to
restrain myself from intervening. I'd watch them with
clenched fists, and sometimes would run to them and make
them come down from the tree, get out of the water. Their
astonished looks were an accusation.

"I'm not afraid," Charles would say. "I'm careful. I
never let go one branch without a good grip on another."

46

Often I would go up ahead of him and break off the dead branches, but when I leaped down to the ground my son's disappointment was obvious.

"I want to go first," he'd say. "By myself."

The child and the man want to measure their strength.
To become what they wish to be and should be, they
must confront the world and things.
Fear and sorrow are good teachers. He who suffers dis-
covers, discovers himself.

And then I did not want my sons and my daughters to be ignorant of the ordeals and joys afforded by the body exercised to its utmost. It was for that reason that we left the city, the universe of slave machines, the sharp air, horizons cut off by concrete walls, uninterrupted by clumps of trees.

I remembered my days in the forests of Europe at war, when we lived with the snow for overcoat, when we reached our red, chapped hands to the embers and the water froze in the pails. Among us were resistance fighters from the city: Bronek the professor, his thin glasses dropping down his nose, always shaking his head, complaining.

"We're living like animals," he'd say. The peasants laughed at him.

"You don't know a thing, Bronek. You've lived off books. Bad for you, paper."

Bronek wandered through the forest with us, lost, as if he'd been transported to another planet. He didn't know how to make a fire, break a branch; he walked with his eyes on the ground for obstacles and stumbled anyway.

The peasants, on the contrary, walked steadily ahead, not minding the drifts or snow-covered trunks that lay a-cross the paths. Then at the last second they would swerve aside as if warned by their whole body. They would leap over the trunk and wait for Bronek, shouting, "Watch out here!"

Even forewarned, Bronek would fall on his face. And yet snow, the forest, nature are part of man's world. With them, against them and thanks to them man has written his history. But some of us have lost our way in this living universe of fields and trees. Thus Bronek, the savant, knew none of the signs which the peasants read in the sky or snow.

He was ignorant of his own body.

The body, the nature in ourselves, that one must know and master.

I watched Bronek as he pushed back a branch with his arm, not lowering his head enough and receiving the branch's cold slap in his face. Didn't he know how tall he was? Did he refuse to this extent to know himself? He was clumsy, ridiculous, always exhausted.

Only at night did he recover his dignity. As the fire crackled he would begin to talk, tell stories, analyze the country's past and describe what was necessary for paradise

48

to be born on this earth. We remained silent, charmed by his ardent voice. Then one of us said with a laugh:

"You talk so well, but it's enough just to see you walk. How do you expect us to believe you? You know nothing about what really exists. The trees. . . ."

Bronek was irritated by these interruptions which sooner or later, whenever he spoke to us, were bound to occur.

"What is there to see? I wasn't born hereabouts. What I am telling you is true, though. . . ."

"You don't even know if it's going to snow tomorrow."

Bronek would get up.

"Imbeciles, imbeciles."

Usually his retreat from the fire was accompanied by laughter.

One after the other we fell asleep. When it was my turn to stand guard, leaning against a trunk in a fur cape, I would think of Bronek and laugh silently. I talked with an imaginary companion, trying to understand. I made a man in my mind who would have the body and instinct of a peasant for whom the forest held no mystery, and who would have known how to guide me as Bronek did in the forest of ideas. But Bronek was ignorant of his body. And the peasants, our comrades, had often been unable to discover anything but the world of fields, the variations of the climate and the maladies and moods of their livestock.

A man must be whole. He is instinct and reason. He

must accept the body and the spirit. The tree is made
of bark and sap. Strip the bark and the tree dies.
If the sap runs dry, the bark rots and the tree dies.
He who wishes only to be the sap and he who knows
only the bark is not truly a man.

I knew that in the city my children would not have been able to discover their bodies, experience the fatigue of muscles, the taste of fruit taken from the trees. They would never have scratched themselves on thorns and would not have learned, by the thin white veil of clouds from the west, the coming of the storm.

And I wanted them to have in themselves this primary knowledge of their bodies confronted by wind, plants, the sky. To discover, when they plunged into the waves and clung to the branches, the resistance of the world, their own strength and their weakness.

Nicole, one day in spring, when the sea is still cold and rough, wanted to go swimming. Our cove was deserted, its red rocks swept fitfully by white foam. But the head of the cove was a pebble beach on which the waves expired. I tried to dissuade Nicole from going in. I had a presentiment. She insisted. We were alone.

"It's important to me," she said. Her face was set, willful. She wanted to test herself. I took off my own clothes.

"Wait."

Already she was running through the foam, and dived into a wave. I saw her between two waves. The water swirled around my legs. Perhaps it was best to stay back. She began to swim out from the shore, beyond the breakers, in the regular swell. I waved to her to come in. I guessed her smile, her joy in testing herself. She swam towards the small beach, riding a wave in. Then just as she was reaching her hand to me, a brutal undertow carried her out again. The cove funnelled each wave that came in. If I'd gone in I too would have been taken out far from the shore.

"Stay out there, don't be afraid."

She waved to me and began floating on her back, out past the seething foam. I bounded up the rocks cursing myself, my having allowed her to do it, my blind weakness. I had a rope in the car. I ran down to the beach again. Nicole was still the same distance from the shore. I waded into the water and threw her the rope. I began pulling and despite the undertow hauled her in. She shivered against me, breathing with difficulty, her lips blanched by the cold.

I silently chafed her.

"Have you understood?" I asked her.

She nodded slightly.

"You cannot do everything. Want everything. I was wrong to let you," I said.

We slowly climbed toward the car, holding each other's hand.

"This little adventure is between you and me. No need to mention it at home."

She pressed my hand more tightly.

"You think about it, and if you decide that it's something

your mother, Suzanne and Charles can hear about, we'll tell them."

I hoped that she would do so.

*Man must accept his errors, must admit his weaknesses.
When one recognizes them they are already half overcome.*

A few days later, Nicole came to me. I was alone on the terrace, looking at the sea.

"Well, I think we'll have to tell them," she said. "Charles always wants to play the fool—he'll learn from this."

At the dinner table, she told the story unemphatically and hiding nothing, now and then looking at me. Afterwards I said,

"That's what happened. We were very careless."

But it's past now," Dina said.

*The past, for a man, should be his experience and what
he has learned from it.*

But sometimes the past is a swamp in which one slowly sinks, where one loses one's way. The past may condemn one to a slow death.

I understood this when I once more found myself alone, my wife and children vanished, my life before me like a desert.

My temptation then, my only desire, was to live in the past, to immure myself in memories.

I saved everything, their toys and their clothing, accordions and schoolbags, all petrified in the lava of misery. I wanted nothing to be touched, wanted everything to be there for my eyes and heart, these objects without life that were its sole trace.

At night, I would sit in the music room and run off all the films and slides that I'd taken of them. I saw them running in the fields, playing beneath the sun-warmed water from an irrigation pipe. I did not weep or cry out in rage. I lived through my eyes as if seeing them, touching things that had been theirs, had brought them back to life. For nearly a month I did the same thing each night. I refused to speak, I felt neither hunger nor thirst; present and future no longer existed. There was only the past.

One night I was overcome by exhaustion. I fell asleep in front of the screen, so quickly that I do not remember lying down. But I had a nightmare which I relived when the sun awoke me. I was in the death camp, which by a miracle I had escaped. But in the dream I was not getting away; the yellow sand of the mass graves which the Germans shoveled over thousands of victims was slowly enveloping me, getting in my mouth and eyes. The gravedigger was emptying his last shovelful, the one that would suffocate me, when I awoke. All morning I wandered through the house, going through my children's rooms, touching the objects that had belonged to them, looking at their beds which I had left just as they were on the day of their disappearance.

Is living shut up in misery being faithful to those one loved?

In the death camp I had known men who, in the name of what they called their faith, allowed themselves to be shovelled under the yellow sand.

The nightmare of the previous evening came back to me. I felt the sand closing over my head.

In the camp, I had managed to escape. Not to forget my dead but to defend them, to witness for them.

And now?

That same day, a neighbor brought me a long letter which the local inhabitants had addressed to the authorities requesting assistance for recovery from the fires in which my family had died.

"A letter?" I said. "Assistance? But that's not enough. More must be done."

At that moment, I decided to create the Foundation for the protection of nature, to stimulate defense against forest fires.

Once more I tried not to let myself be obliterated by the past but to remain faithful to it by making it serve as a springboard.

A man's past can be like a plant growing wild in the field or climbing a wall.
It can stifle young shoots, or it can loosen the heaviest stones.

The past can be evil for a man.

Man can neither deny nor efface the past. He carries its inscription in him always. It is his unique, personal history.

But he must lean on it, learn from it.

To use his experience as a support to gain his distance from the past without either betraying or forgetting it.

For life is a progress towards the future. One must trust in whatever comes.

Often, during the war, or later in the great cities I frequented on business, I knew men who were hostile to me from the start. Some stripped me of my goods, others betrayed me. They were well aware that when they robbed me it meant hunger, that their betrayals sent me to my death. And those who in peacetime prevented me from selling because it crimped their trade, what were they condemning me to but misery?

How could I trust these men who had declared war on me? Nevertheless, one day, out of need and defiance, I joined with these people, these enemies.

"Here I am," I told them.

I spoke to their self-interest rather than their feelings, the solidarity that should exist between men. I had no hope that they would shed themselves of their practices, their past.

We began taking our risks together, bringing sacks of

wheat into the starving ghetto, fleeing together, fighting together. And gradually these people, whom I'd thought a
mixture of mud and hate, became my comrades.

> *There is always the chance that a man is better than he*
> *appears.*
> *One must discover in a man the path that leads to his*
> *profound source. One must help him to be reborn.*
> *Then a man stands up in him. The real one.*
> *For man, if he is bound to the past, is also a future life.*

I had a long talk with one of the members of the gang
whom I'd collected around me during the war. Often we
had to hole up together for hours at a stretch. I questioned
him.

"Mokotow, why are you this way?"

"What way?"

"A thief."

He shrugged his shoulders and smiled.

"Who isn't a thief?" he asked me. "I have to live."

"But you could have chosen something else. . . ."

He cut me short, unsmiling. He lay back, his hands
under his head.

"Who told you I didn't try?"

"Why aren't you still trying?"

"The war. . . ."

"The war will end, and then you can do it."

"You think so?"

There was hope in his voice. I sensed that part of him that was still fresh, which his history as a man and History had not yet deformed.

"I am sure that you can begin again."

"You think so?" he repeated.

In almost all men there is an unchangeable element buried in their nature.
To find it, you must believe that it is there.

Mokotow became my friend.

He separated himself from those who, because no one had spoken to them, continued to be ignorant of themselves in a violent life. He helped me. He fought as a good man does.

I looked for him in vain when I returned to the city with the victorious army. Where was he? Perhaps he died a martyr under the white dust of the ruins, a defiant smile on his lips.

When man is revealed to himself, when man has once listened to the source that is in him, who can say how far he will go?

I have often thought of Mokotow.

Long afterwards, when I had already achieved my third

life, the life of happiness, I discovered this motto of a
medieval city: "More is in you." Then I understood
Mokotow.

More is in man.

I know that this motto is true.

But when war engulfed me, I did not know man's pow-
ers of resistance. I did not know that man's spirit can be a
diamond which nothing can break.

I saw those men who reentered their prison cells after
torture without having let a cry of agony or any information
escape them.

I felt my will hardening under blows.

The more my body seemed ready to burst, my skin to
rend, the more I felt my being concentrate, gather its
strength. The torturers' blows were meant to efface me from
the world, and I felt that I was being born.

They wanted to destroy even the memory of my people;
I felt that it would arise stronger than ever.

My hope was realized. My people were dispersed. Per-
secutions brought them back to their source.

Ordeal, for a man, is the means of knowing himself and
of growing.
Suffering, misery, and injustice make that diamond
shine in the heart of the real man.
They defeat only that man who has nothing in himself.

I have something in myself. I do not pride myself on it. It is from others—my father, my mother, the good men I have known, and deeper inside myself my race that has made its history my own, have made me what I am. They have given me strength and hope.

Thanks to them all, I have put down deep roots. I have bark and sap. I have recognized my source, and the waters of origin continue to nourish me. I have loved life. I still love it.

I have learned to want to be myself. Slowly I have tamed those savage forces that exist in every being. I have accepted their presence and tried not to capitulate to them.

They broke loose in me and against me when I was once more alone, deprived forever of those I loved. They nearly prevailed. I came near to committing suicide.

Perhaps I have reached the beginning of a fourth life.

A life which will deny none of my former lives, which will not be composed of forgetfulness and negation of the past.

To grow, for a man, is never to forget what has been but to know it, and detach yourself from it in order to better see yourself and the goal.
And the goal of man is to be himself.
Because to be yourself is to go toward others. As the spring goes toward the sea.

MAN
ALONE

The sea seems so distant sometimes.

Since I have been alone I've often spent long hours leaning on the brick wall that borders the terrace of the house.

When the warm weather came, Dina and I would take the children down to the beach. It was our daily expedition into the land of noise, the world of the crowd, of traffic jams by the sea.

Now I studied it from here, a blue-grey misty expanse. I was waiting for the red sun's immolation in it. I stood unmoving, fascinated by the devouring sea.

I was alone.

I had been alone many times before. In prison, anticipating my imminent death. In forests, when I was fleeing the death camp.

And also, alone with others.

In the city with its long streets, the gleaming steel of cars, the dusty wind blowing in the canyons of the skyscrapers. Alone among those men and women who jostled me.

Like myself, alone.

Shoulder to shoulder we descended subway stairs, crowded into elevators without looking at each other.

One day, jammed against the back wall of an elevator, I felt a growing anguish within me. I thought it was due to the heat, the lack of air, a confused fear at being far from the doors behind twenty people of whom I saw only their backs.

Margaret, my friend then, told me that she had a dread of being trapped in a crowd, that she preferred not to enter a full compartment, a theatre with few empty seats. She laughed:

"I stifle, I panic, I have to leave. It's the same thing in planes, often. . . ."

I didn't take her seriously. I had ridden cattle cars en route to the inferno, in which we were already dying. I had wormed through sewers to get to the free zone to buy arms. I had learned to master the fear one experiences in a subterranean tunnel half-filled with water. I never expected to feel as Margaret did.

"My throat constricts," she explained. She put her hand around her throat.

"It's as if someone had taken me by the throat. I can tell many of my friends are like myself. My mother has the same feelings."

"Modern times," I said laughing. "Besides, you're women."

Margaret shrugged her shoulders. And with good reason.

And now as we ascended in the elevator I, too, who had taken pride in self-control, was seized by the irrational fear that Margaret had described to me.

Finally the doors opened and I jostled my way out. Slowly making my way among the various departments of the store, I thought about what had happened to me.

What did this anguish come from? Why had it over-whelmed me after so many others? Why didn't my mind maintain its defenses, prevent this tide of anxiety, this heat rising in the throat?

I went out onto the street. It was growing dark and misty. Hurried groups of employees were coming out of offices, swarming across the avenues and disappearing into the subways.

The anguish that had taken me, that Margaret had also experienced, was not merely a physical phenomenon. The sweat that had bathed my brow was not merely from the heat.

What I had felt, what we all had felt more or less accord-ing to our fatigue and health, was *the solitude among others*.

I had not been aware of it in the elevator, but those backs in front of me and round bodies, those men and women jammed against each other, not speaking to each other, not looking at each other, who did not know each other and who would never see each other again, what were

they for me and for each other but the proof that we did not
exist for each other, that we were each alone in this crowd?
And how could we, feeling with our whole bodies that we
were strangers to each other, not have been afraid, not have
felt attacked, wounded, destroyed in the deepest part of
ourselves?

*Men who ignore each other's presence are like stones
heaped together. Man alone is as hard and sterile as a
stone in the field.*

I stayed out on the terrace a long time. I did not go
inside even when night had fallen. Often Madame Sluton
would call to me from the road:
"Since you're out, Monsieur Gray, why not come with
me?"
She was an energetic woman who for some years had
lived alone in a little house just outside the village. Once or
twice a year her daughter would come for a brief visit.
Sometimes when I passed her house with Dina and the
children we would see her and say hello. She would be
seated beneath an olive tree with piles of books around her.
With the book she was reading, she'd wave back happily.
"She's always alone," said Suzanne. "How does she do
it? Who does she talk to?" Dina explained the books, her
daughter. . . .
"She almost never comes," Suzanne said.
After the forest fire and the disappearance of my family,
I rediscovered Madame Sluton.

"Come along with me, Monsieur Gray."

I joined her on the road where she was waiting for me, leaning on her thick wooden cane. We walked slowly along, and she said:

"Do you know Miguel? He didn't want his injection today. These people are extraordinary. Miguel, the poacher—you know he fought in the war—is afraid of an injection."

These casual conversations revealed Madame Sluton to me. She worked as a charity nurse in the village. She saw to it that patients obeyed the rules, lectured mothers who neglected their children, advised the fathers.

"Tell me about yourself, Monsieur Gray." But she gave me no time to answer.

"Do you know that I read something today, and it reminded me of you? A page in the Old Testament, yes. . . ."

Another evening, she told me about a scientific discovery that could revolutionize the treatment of cancer. She was enthusiastic:

"Imagine, an end to the useless suffering from cancer. There is so much to be done still, Monsieur Gray. You don't know what joy I feel when I hear of such a victory. It moves the world."

She took my arm.

"It makes me happy, Martin, because I know that there is, always, something new under the sun. It thrills me."

She made me enter her house. I sat down in the little kitchen.

"I am going to make you some tea."

There were magazines and books on the table. Often, we had scarcely sat down when a child would knock at the door.

"Madame Sluton. . . ."

She was always being asked to do something, to lend a book or some money, or to give an injection. Madame Sluton put on a thick wool jacket. Her wrinkled face beaming, she said:

"Excuse me . . . help yourself and wait if you like. You can see I don't have a moment."

Sometimes I would go out with her, sometimes wait for her or go back alone. I thought of the solitude I had known in the city, experienced by so many people; the solitude that terrifies, that they fought with drugs and television. And I thought of Madame Sluton, who lived alone and yet who was never alone.

Man can be alone among others. But he who is open to the world, who retains a fraternal solidarity with others, even though he is alone he is not lonely.

Because others, when a hand is held out to them, will take it.

Man is never alone in his aloneness. He can always find someone to go through life with him.

Often in the past, I had despaired of that helping hand—in the inferno, the death camp.

The executioners were animals with men's faces, and the victims seemed to accept their fate.

In peace also I had had this fear, the fear of being alone.

Fear, because if one is alone, what use is there in living?

Then I discovered that it was I who had constructed this prison, this solitude and this fear. That I had been unable to see the hand held out to me.

The immurement in one's self, that dungeon, is a deadly poison. It breeds fear and isolation.

In Treblinka, when I traversed the courtyard where our executioners sorted us out, making us undress before they sent us to our deaths, I saw prisoners who risked their lives to whisper advice to a newly arrived man so he would have his chance. But during the first days I did not guess their courage; I judged from the appearances, isolated in my false certainties. I had imagined that in this hell man could not but be alone.

A few weeks later and without a word, my life was saved by these men, who in so doing gave theirs.

After I had fled the camp a peasant gave me some bread at the edge of a field. The bread of brotherhood.

Later, in another prison, a man in the enemy's uniform saved me from summary execution. The look he gave me saved me from despair.

Another person's glance can shatter solitude. And it will come. But one must believe that it exists.

Those who were the first to succumb in that barbarous war to fear and then to death, those who gave up, were those who lived their life as men alone. Those whose world was limited to their bodies.

My father had told me, "You must live, be a witness. You must revenge our people and continue it."

Thus I was much more than myself.

I walked alone in the forest looking for combatants and I felt no fatigue. When I was lined up against the wall to be shot, I dived down the airhole of a cellar. To escape I accepted having to squat in excrement.

Did I have more courage than others? Of course, I was young. But above all I had the feeling of being a small necessary part of a great whole, my immortal people. I could not give in. I was no longer reduced to myself. I was not alone.

I remember one encounter at winter's end, at the edge of a forest when snow still lay on the fields and the sky, low and heavy, seemed to cling to the trees.

They were two young men—I'd heard their voices, the sound of the branches they broke, and I followed them cautiously. Then I realized that they were speaking my language, and caught up with them. They whirled around, first afraid then joyful.

"Where are you from?"

I explained how I'd fled and how I was heading for the capital to fight with the remnants of my people against the Germans.

"Come with me."

I urged them to come back with me to the battle. They looked at each other. The youngest, his black hair curly over his forehead, listened to me with shining eyes. The elder nibbled at the long nails of his frost-reddened fingers.

"No," he said. "No. We escaped in winter. We've survived so far, and we're going to stay here."

I went on talking. But I'd learned to judge people; I knew when they would obey or resist. The younger would take the elder's advice. The latter would not change his mind.

I said, "We have to go back with the others, for ourselves and them."

"So long," said the elder brother.

"And the others?"

He laughed.

"You know what they are, those others," he said. "Mad beasts. Cowards too." I left them, I took to the woods again. I didn't have time to convince them. An hour lost meant less of life for my people. I went quickly. I pushed the branches out of my way, the snow falling like white dust.

I turned to look at them. I saw them standing still, refusal. And so weak, so vulnerable, two defenseless, meager bodies.

While I was strong with the assurance of hope of a whole people, of its desire to fight and survive.

> *A man is never alone when he knows that he is the tiny
> yet necessary part of a whole, a powerful, innumera-
> ble whole: the collectivity of men.*
> *A man is never alone when he does not make himself the
> unique goal of his life.*
> *A man is never alone, a man is never weak when he
> mingles his energy in the immense ocean of human
> energies.*

I had never understood this better than after the death of
my family.

My life became possible again from that moment when I
reemerged from myself, when I no longer contemplated my
sorrow except to use it for others and in my family's memory.

> *Man cannot escape sorrow and solitude except when he
> knows there is a man more unfortunate and more
> alone than himself.*
> *A man who is waiting for a hand to be reached to him.*

At first this was not easy. Then I had the idea of this
foundation which would fight against the destruction of nature, against forest fires and pollution.

No longer was I a man alone, stricken by an outrageous
fate. I'd become a fighter again; I had a cause that was more
than myself, I was of use, I was a man among men and my
sorrow rather than isolating me joined me to them.

Some failed to understand me. The important official who received me in his office shook his head as he spoke to me.

"Mr. Gray, I respect you, I sympathize with you in your loss, your indignation, but what can we do? You are a man alone, and you hope to succeed where powerful organizations have failed?"

I was not alone, since I had decided to turn to others. And I knew that they would come to me.

The skeptical official did not dissuade me, and he was wrong.

A few weeks later there gathered in front of my house, on that lawn which the fire had scorched, a group comprised of local mayors, journalists, important people and also simple men. They all shared my wish, to prevent the recurrence of a tragedy similar to mine—the destruction of lives and forests by fire. I spoke to them; I was no longer alone, we were a group with a common goal.

One of the last to leave was the official, who had been sent by his superior as an "observer." He gave me a long handshake.

"You are extraordinary," he said. "I could have sworn that you would fail."

Extraordinary? It was he who had failed to understand the strength that one can find in others when one goes to them.

"I told myself," he continued, still holding my hand, "that if I were in your place I would lodge a complaint so that a court inquiry could establish responsibility. One should know whose fault it was, surely."

I listened to him. If I'd followed that course it would have led me into a solitude even more arid. What I had to do was prevent the recurrence of such dramas, the flames rising up around the hills. For this purpose it was necessary to turn not to the past but the future. Not to find the guilty but allies.

> *To accuse others is to shut yourself up in self. To condemn yourself to be alone.*
> *The other is not necessarily an enemy but a possible ally.*
> *And perhaps even he who opposes you can help you. We should always learn something from our adversary.*

And since my foundation was established I have found everywhere men and women who came to me, willing to help.

It was they who gave me the strength to speak, for I understood that my voice could open the circle of solitude in which they were often enclosed, could break the stone that crushed them. I had believed in them. They believed in me.

> *One must have faith in people.*

So often in my life I have confided in a person, sometimes by a simple look, all my chances in life. And I was right.

I have begun again.

When I met the writer Max Gallo with whom I would collaborate on my life's story, *For Those I Loved,* I did not know him. But it needed but a few words to know that through him I would reach others, that he would find those simple words that would tell readers my story. I spoke to him each day for months, his face immobile, turned toward me, only his hand moving over the paper.

Sometimes when I left him, I'd be attacked by anxiety.

"Will you be able to make all this understood?" I asked him.

It was terrible, yet I had the hope, the fear and the hope, that the reader must understand.

We shook hands and a few days later, when he read me what he'd written, I seemed to hear my own voice, the language in order, in a faithful text. I knew then that the book would be a step toward others, that between the readers and myself the same tie would exist as between myself and Max Gallo. That this book, *For Those I Loved,* would not merely be one more book but that through it I would meet men and women, that we would no longer be alone.

When the book was published, I discovered immediately that I had not been mistaken. I had spoken with my heart, Max Gallo had written with his. The readers could not but understand what we had wished to say.

For another to hear you, for him to come to you and for solitude to end, one must be true, go forward unarmed, with the invincible strength of fraternity. Then dialogue is born.
And the dialogue of a man with others is life.

I began to receive letters from readers, thousands of letters. Max Gallo and I were surprised. Neither of us had imagined the fullness of the echo which a message without hate always finds in man.

I read these letters. Some began with these words: "My friend, my brother." I remember one for its childish handwriting: "Come to us," this thirteen-year-old reader said, "come, don't be alone on Christmas. You will like it in our house, you won't be alone."

How could I be alone when each of my readers told me of his faith in me, of how my book had brought him comfort and courage, and when each ended with the question: "What can I do for you?"

Then I visited the great cities. In the full conference rooms and bookstores, I saw the emotion in people's eyes. I knew that I had been understood. That he had been wrong, that neighbor who when I'd spoken to him of my intentions to create a foundation and publish a book had shaken his head.

"People will think the worst," he kept saying. "They're naturally malicious, they'll say you're doing it for fame and maybe even money. That's how they are. Travel, forget, don't speak of it; change your life. One is always disappointed in others."

He who believes à priori in others' hostility is himself alone.

I was no longer alone.

At Lausanne, I spent an entire afternoon in a big store inscribing copies of *For Those I Loved.* One after the other, men and women came up to me, shook my hand, asked me to talk to them. In the evening, without its having been arranged, Max Gallo and I held a public conference in a hotel.

The small room was badly lit; I stood leaning against a table. I had the impression that I was not finding the words I should use but I tried to say what was in me. I finished, there were a few questions, and then someone rose and said:

"I would like all of us to observe tonight a minute of silence for all those who disappeared in the holocaust, and for those whom Martin Gray loved."

In that room we were not like stones in a heap ignorant of each other, we were like the different branches of one tree. We suffered together and we remembered those branches the storm had torn away.

One must learn to share the sufferings of others. Then they will give you their joys. And one will no longer be alone.

Thus, Madame Vincent. She came to the office of the
Foundation. A small woman with a set face, dressed in
black and carrying a handbag.

"I would like to help you," she said with a kindly ex-
pression.

She said nothing more, merely standing before me and
my collaborators. We had no need of a secretary yet hesitated to send her away.

"I can do anything you like," she said.

I accepted her offer. She came punctually every day
before anyone else, sitting in a corner of the office copying
addresses, silent, devoted. I finally learned that she had
seen the car in which her husband and son were riding
catch fire. Her husband was dead. Her son was in the hospital, in a coma. He was not expected to live. She was not
allowed to visit him.

She came to the Foundation to help others and escape
her misery.

To help others is the best way to help one's self.

One evening when I was leaving the office, I saw
Madame Vincent alone at her desk, her chin propped on
her palms, the tears pouring down her face.

"Is something the matter?"

Not answering, she shook her head.

"Then. . . ."

"I think he's gone," she said.

She had called the hospital, and they had given her very little hope for her son's recovery.

"But no, no. . . ."

I tried to convince myself in order to convince her.

"I'm leaving," she said.

She stood up, slowly gathering her coat and bag.

"I shouldn't talk this way to you, who have so much more reason than I to despair and yet have not lost courage."

I accompanied her to her home. We spoke to each other, gradually revealing our personal miseries. We evoked life, others. She listened to me and I listened to her.

"I used to believe in God," she said. "Now I don't know. I didn't deserve to see what I did. Or if I'd committed some sin why my husband, my son? Why him, so young, so innocent. How can I believe in God?"

"I don't know. . . ."

God. That was also one of my questions. Many had found in Him, and thanks to Him, peace. They were no longer alone. He spoke to them. And even His silence was an answer. For me it was enough if I could go out to others, living beings, and with or without faith, to respect and help them. As if they were, each of them, creatures of God.

In front of her home, Madame Vincent grasped my hand tightly.

"I was going to kill myself," she said. "Tonight."

I took her by the shoulders.

"You're mad."

She smiled sadly.

"Sometimes I think I am, when I think of what has happened to me. Of what I've seen. Why not die?"

I still held her shoulders. I could feel her trembling.

"And now? You're not going. . . ."

"It's past," she said. "I'll be better now. I think I'll be able to sleep."

Sometimes a word, a look is enough to avoid the irreparable. Or provoke it.

One must be attentive to others. To their silent appeals.

To imagine at all times that someone has an indispensable need of you to loosen the solitude which is strangling him.

Madame Vincent came to the office the next morning and all the days following.

A few weeks later, I had to leave the country. When I visited the Foundation on my return, Madame Vincent was at her desk. The minute she saw me she leaped up and hurried over to me.

"Monsieur Gray," she said, "he's going to be well. . . ."

Her son had emerged from the coma the week before. He would be saved. He would not be blind as had been feared.

I embraced her, her joy entered me and became my own, gave me a strength which I'd needed today, against the sadness which had invaded me on my return to Paris, a city I had visited often with my wife Dina.

"I owe it to you," Madame Vincent said. "You remember that night when you accompanied me back, you spoke to me so well. . . . I don't know what I would have done without you. Perhaps. . . ." Her joy protected me from my pain.

He who gives receives.

I left Paris for my house in the South a few days later. By car—the necessary attention and gestures required by driving were for me, when assailed by sad memories, a way of resisting them. And since nothing is as simple as one says it is, despite the Foundation, despite the letters of my readers, I often felt alone. As for Madame Vincent, it had fallen to me to struggle against despair without certainty of victory.

At the approaches to the highway there were groups of young people hitchhiking, with names of cities to the south inscribed on pieces of cardboard. I slowed down. A little back from the road there was a couple sitting, she with long blond hair and a kind of green knit blanket over her shoulders, and he with curly shoulder-length hair and a guitar under his arm. I stopped. Why not give them a lift?

Often I'd passed them in the cities, bands of young people dressed in dirty, extravagant clothes, the uniform of
youth.

Once I'd searched with Dina in mountain villages for
the teenage son of friends, who had disappeared leaving
the simple message: "I'm going on the road to be free." And
yet no one had been given more freedom than he had.

By chance we found him near the frontier, sitting on a
milestone. A miracle.

I tried to question him. His face was shut, silent, not
looking at me and occasionally answering with a curse.
When we returned him to his parents he scarcely greeted
them. His mother cried and laughed, constantly saying,
"Why, but why?" He went directly to his room.

The young couple came toward my car. I opened the
back door for them and they got in. The young man kept his
guitar on his knees, while the young girl took the green
blanket from her shoulders.

I drove, studying them in the mirror. Were they running
away from home like my friends' son? They had not so
much as thanked me for the lift. Perhaps they were politely
waiting for me to open the conversation. But I felt no wish
to talk; I preferred to watch them in the mirror, observing in
their faces that malaise of big city living: the unhappiness
and solitude of youth. It was a serious malaise.

For solitude breeds violence and despair.

I remembered my surprise, as I drove through certain

parts of cities, at young people leaning against shop fronts with hands in their pockets, sitting on the curb or running like young dogs to retrieve balls or jam-tins they were playing with. There they were, victims of their solitude. That they went in groups made no difference, since each retained his solitude within the group. The parents and also their elder brothers and sisters were at the office. So they wandered, lost in the dirty streets of the sprawling metropolis.

My youth had been subject to the laws of war, hunger and death. In a sense I found it to have been less desperate than theirs. I knew what I had to fight, and I knew who my allies were. I knew why I had to fight: for the survival of my people and to revenge those I'd loved. In my misery I had a pole star to guide me.

For he who is animated by an ideal, who shares in a grand collective design, is not alone.

But these teenagers of cities at peace, this young man clutching his guitar and this young woman leaning her head against the window, what would encourage them to become adults? To live? Sometimes, when I saw these young people straying along the avenues, lying on the beaches or sitting side by side, they reminded me of frenzied bees in search of an exit, banging against the walls of a fishbowl, or else they were like stones that are thrown away, roll a little and then stop.

Of course, peace was better than war. In war youth was

annihilated, martyred. But were they living in peace, these adolescents, or were they engaged in implacable warfare within? A war whose nature they did not know but which forced them to act, to leave their families, to take to drugs and violence. Each of them was, without knowing it, his own executioner and victim.

The violence of a person alone is primarily directed against himself.

And they were alone, these young people, too often alone.

In the besieged city I had known during the war, I was less alone than they. Even if many of us trapped in the city thought only of ourselves, I knew myself that we shared a common destiny. That I was part of a whole.

But these boys and girls shut in these gloomy streets, growing up in this metallic universe in which each was isolated in the nickeled cabin of his car, how could they feel they belonged to a whole?

They tried to recreate solidarity—they gathered, they sang together, danced and took drugs together. But how could bodily groupings and encounters satisfy them?

One does not cease to be alone in a group.
One remains alone unless one participates in a great common enterprise.

"What are you going to do down there?" I asked, looking around at them.

The girl shrugged her shoulders. The young man laughed.

"Same thing as here, nothing, except there'll be sun down there. We'll be warm." He put his arm around the shoulders of the girl, who moved away as if to avoid contact. That was it. They were fleeing solitude in provisional, fragile pairings. It was no solution.

We must each first wish to conquer ourselves, the loneliness within ourselves.

My passengers didn't exchange more than a few words throughout the trip. They made me think of those couples tired of being a couple, side by side in lifelong mutual solitude. They were young but they behaved like tired, bored adults.

They got out at the exit of the highway. I watched them going off, he dangling his guitar, and she putting the blanket over her shoulders again.

For two people to find each other, to destroy each his own solitude by the other, they must share their future.

To reach my house in les Barons from the highway I had to

take a narrow road that climbed a hill and then entered the
charred forest in which my family had perished. The children of the village, by the road where Dina had attempted
to escape, where the car shrouded in smoke had skidded
down the slope, had erected a stone with the names of my
children, their ex-playmates, inscribed on it.

I slowed down and stopped, as always. I walked toward
the slope, fascinated by those burned trunks of which some
were already covered with green moss—life that went on
stronger than fire. I sat down. Before me were little valleys
and rocky slopes, an arid landscape. In the distance the
highway, the first houses, the town by the sea.

The cause of the fire had never been precisely ascer-
tained. A smoker's carelessness? A camper? Perhaps a spark
from the high tension cables strung from pole to pole which
brushed the tops of the trees? Or perhaps the sun shining
on a bit of glass that served as a magnifying lens, with the
fire taking on the dry earth at the close of a rainless season,
spread by the wind. I looked at this martyred nature. All
along the highway were open wounds inflicted by man.
Hills cut into, fields and trees covered with white dust from
a factory chimney. Just outside Paris, I stopped at a parking
lot in a forest. Walking along a path I found excrement,
bottles, cans, papers, wooden and paper boxes, traces left
by man. The evil he was committing against nature.

And here before me was burned earth, stones sundered
and blackened. This fire which, whatever the details, man
had caused.

Why all this evil? This disorder that man introduced into nature, plundering and mutilating, unaware that the damage he inflicted would one day boomerang against him?

Man is not alone on this earth. He is but one part of nature. If he destroys it, he will find himself alone in a desert.

When I bought les Barons I took a walk with an old peasant on the hills that ringed my property.

Bent, with his hands to his back, wearing a straw hat deeply gashed at its brim that hid his face burned brown by a lifetime in the sun, he walked ahead of me.

"They used to grow wheat here," he told me.

He pointed to the narrow strips of terraced earth that climbed the hill like stairs.

"And now, stones. It was good earth before they began cutting down trees, and the rain washed it away. Now. . . ." He bent over and picked up a handful of sharp-edged stones. "This is what's left."

At that time, more than ten years ago, I was a different person. I answered the peasant that work on these far hills was exhausting, that wheat nowadays grew on the great plains traversed by machines as ships plough the sea. The old peasant shrugged.

"You don't understand, Monsieur Gray, it's not a question of the work. Growing wheat here was like having a child by the earth. One respected the earth; it was the mother. Today, thanks to our cleverness the earth is dead; there's nothing but stones."

I laughed at him. It seemed to me that man was well advised to leave the difficult regions, to abandon hard work in the fields. I imagined that one day machines would do everything.

I had chosen nature myself, I had left the city, but this seemed to me merely a personal solution. If I loved nature I did not understand its importance. I loved it above all as a pleasant habitat, gentler to the eye than the gray facades of cities.

I took up life at les Barons. I planted peach trees, I picked the heavy fruit with my children, I bit into the sugary flesh. I walked barefoot through the tall grass, and with my children climbed trees, ran and slept under the sun. I understood that nature was not a decor. I loved it like a living being with many faces. And when the fire came, when my family died, when I walked for whole nights among the still-smouldering stumps, blackening my clothes with the charred branches, then I saw it clearly. I experienced the union of man and nature and the sadness of man in a ravaged nature.

If man feels himself to be alone, if anguish and fear inhabit him, it is because he has cut his ties with nature.

But this union can be happy. I had known it to be so for ten years, with my family. In the harmony of sunsets at sea, in the songs of birds that awakened us all in the mornings. I would go out and walk barefoot on the dewy lawn.

After the fire, the birds deserted the hills. I saw the forest dead. I thought of all those parts of the world that have become dusty wastelands. There where meadows had been, man had substituted gray heaps of sterile earth that the wind played with. And it was for this, for this plundered nature that I wished to create the Dina Gray Foundation, to preserve and protect man's environment. Not for nature itself nor only for man, but for the whole which they form together.

Man and nature form a whole which lives but may die.
Separately, each becomes a sterile stone.
If man ignores or destroys nature, he ignores and destroys himself.

I understand now that one of the causes of my former anguish was that living in great cities, going on business from one capital to another, I had no time to discover nature. Of course my anxiety had other causes. I doubted if I would meet a woman I loved, who would become the one companion of my life. But above all there was the prison of living in an overly large city. It stifled me.

Nowhere could I find the calm of a field that stretched to

the horizon—nowhere the grasses bowing under a breeze,
the mauve colors of a sunset dying behind trees, the noises
that gradually blended with the light. None of that which
here at les Barons, in this now tragic setting before the destroyed forest in which my loved ones perished, remains
and soothes me despite all, despite its past and ravaged
nature. The city was noise, harsh air, crowds, mask-like
faces. Aggression and fatigue had become so much a part of
life that they passed unnoticed. Now, I was able to compare. To understand how the city is a jungle in which each
is alone. When as a young immigrant I climbed the stairs of
apartment houses in the Bronx to sell my wares, I was
struck even then by the fear I read in people's eyes when
they came to the door. Often I had to slip a foot inside the
frame so they wouldn't close it in my face.

*Fear and solitude, as if each unknown person might be
an enemy.*

In the city too big for its own good, such are the laws of
these groupings of millions of people who cannot but live
in self-ignorance.

Man is never as alone as in a crowd.

I remember the derelict whom I invariably encountered
on my trips to Paris, lying on the sidewalk ventilation grill
of the subway near my hotel. I would arrive back from New

York or Berlin, London or Rome, and there I would find him enveloped in his black cloak as if he hadn't budged for a week. I passed near him, and thousands of others hurried by him.

Did they see him? Did they know he was a man?

I could not but think of other reclining forms I'd seen by the thousands in my starving city, the skeleton-like emblems of wartime. Now it was peacetime but there were still these men and women, abandoned in the gutters of a capital. Often they were old, human wreckage which life, ill fortune and hazard had left to die with indifference.

There is no worse solitude than that produced by others' indifference. Each of us may at some time be the victim of indifference and suffer for it. Why do we not hold our hand out to him who is alone?

I know. There is no time. I myself passed that derelict by without more than a glance which registered that the snow was slowly covering him, that he was doubtless drunk. Then I went on my way; I had business. Today I ask myself if these unfortunate, solitary men and women that one sees, these old forgotten people in their chilly apartments where the worst cold is their own solitude, are not warnings, images of what we should not forget, of what we may become.

No one can say that one day he will not be a man alone.

But how could one think of this?

I was busy in my affairs and projects, and then there was my meeting Dina, my children. Perhaps my happiness blinded me. I had forgotten that it could only be temporary. But how was I to imagine that what I had constructed could be destroyed in a single day?

Since I have been once more alone, I know better that life is full of shocks. That no one can say that he will escape the misery of being alone.

Solitude is a mirror; we discover ourselves in it, what we have been and what we are.

Solitude is a trial.

Only he who has not exhausted the source in himself can emerge from it the victor. Solitude reveals the true man.

Sometimes it is necessary to seek it, sometimes it is unavoidable, implacable.

After I escaped from the death camp, on the roads and in the cities spared as yet, I met my brothers, the men and women of my people. When I tried to tell them what I had seen, what was coming, when I tried to convince them they would have to fight, I was not understood. I was taken for a fool, a young fanatic.

And I remained alone with my certainty.

He who knows is often alone. But this loneliness is

the price one must pay for what he knows.
And one must accept it with head high and firm
heart.

I left them after doing everything in my power to warn
my people of the barbarism that was about to engulf them.

It was hard to leave them, to abandon them to their
tranquil ignorance. What should I do, die with them or flee
alone in order to fight for them?

It is sometimes necessary to choose solitude, if it is
the only way to remain faithful to yourself and
others.

I have often had to accept it.

Perhaps that is why today, alone again, I am able to
continue. Perhaps because I know also, having lived it, that
love exists. That solitude can have an end.

That love can transform a rocky terrain into a living
and fertile land.

LOVE

B ehind the wall of my terrace, no one could see us. Dina and I often wished to be alone, to see nothing but the sky when we lay out on the sun-scorched cement.

Our children, when the heat was at its height, would be sleeping. We lay side by side. There was silence, the cicadas and sometimes the wind in the nearby trees. Nothing else.

Often friends would visit us. Arriving from New York or Paris, they would enthuse over the landscape, the calm. Then, coming up to the wall, one of them would shake his head and say:

"But you're very alone here. Aren't you bored?"

Dina and I would smile. Boredom—what was that?

When one loves, the other is a universe that one never finishes exploring.
It is the water that quenches thirst, and the thirst that gives the desire to drink.

I understand the man or woman who has a fear of si-

lence, of leaving the city, of finding themselves alone with
another they do not love, or not enough. I have known this
same fear myself. At that time I was living with Margaret.
There was affection and friendship between us. But we
both knew that this was not love. I had always nourished a
hope that one day, like a burst of light in myself, I would
meet the woman whom I would recognize at once, whom I
wanted to live with forever. A woman who would give me
inner peace and joy. And I was not the only one to have this
hope. Who does not have it?

> *Each of us waits for love. One must keep hoping for its
> coming. For thinking of it opens the way to it.*

I was not going to resign myself to a marriage without
love, a rational union based on understanding alone. And
who can resign himself? Later, when I received friends in
my house at les Barons, I could see quite easily those who
lacked love, who had accepted resignation. There was
Martha whom Dina had known in New York—Martha
whose two sons lived with their wives in cities on the west
coast of the United States. At 47, Martha found herself once
more alone with her husband. Years had passed, her days
had been full with her children, and today she stood alone
on that road which remained to travel with her husband
Jack, a man whom she had hardly seen over the years and
who now was constantly with her.

"I am alone," she repeated to Dina.

They were in the kitchen. I stayed back with Jack.

"Martha isn't doing well," he told me. "The children are away, married, and she's getting older. It's not easy for a woman."

I understood that there was not that love between them that gives confidence.

Love is giving to another the security which one receives in return.

Martha confided her troubles in Dina, the life which she had not seen slip away.

"How can I go on?" she asked. "I can't sleep—you don't know this anguish like a heavy lump in my chest."

Dina and I did know it, having lived a long time without love. But both of us had refused to build a life, a whole life, with a companion who brought us scarcely more than friendship. We had hoped, we had believed in the possibility of love and we had met each other. Martha did not have this certainty in herself; she had fallen into marriage with Jack on account of her youth and other factors. Perhaps also because she'd been afraid of loneliness, and had wanted a ready future for herself, an arm to lean on. She'd thought to gain by it the tranquillity, the two children, the sweet years she had spent watching them grow. Now she had to pay for it.

Life without love is nothing.

And she did not love Jack. She had tenderness but also resentment for him, reproaches which she made as if he'd been responsible for her choice, for the time that had fled, the anguish that weighed on her. Dina tried to make her understand that she had her two children, that her life had meaning because they were living, that Jack who loved her was also there. Martha shook her head, seeming not to hear, as if her life had been merely a desert, as if truly she were alone.

> *When one gives up love for something one takes to be good sense, when one forgets that life is an act of love, a day will come when one discovers that one has wasted it.*
> *Life is earned only when one loves.*

Jack and I went out and walked down the road. My children ran before us, one of them clinging to my arm now and then. Jack would take their hand, and we'd lift and swing Nicole or Charles between us. The children laughed.

"When Martha had her children," said Jack, "she was different. But what do we have to say to each other now? In the evening there's television, and friends visit. Maybe Martha needs something to distract her."

Jack questioned me as if I were a man of great experience, but he was older than myself. What could I answer? He warned me that a day would come when, our children having grown up, Dina and I would find ourselves face to face, alone.

"That will be a difficult moment. Nobody escapes it," he said.

I was sure that I would not know his anguish. Sure that Dina would not become another Martha. We had chosen each other in enthusiasm. With one look we had understood that each was for the other—joy, liberty and strength.

Love is never constraint.
It is joy, liberty, strength.
And it is love that slays anguish.

I knew this. I had only to remember the time before Dina when I wandered alone in New York, or when I went from one capital to another. I had money, success. I had merely to wish for a woman to meet one. But in fact I was alone. I was building nothing with these chance acquaintances. I was living false joys with them.

Where love is not, boredom and fear are born.

Yes, I was afraid, afraid that I would not meet the woman I desired to be the mother of my longed-for children. Fear—at times I was tempted to accept imperfect solutions, and then something in me would rise up in revolt. I knew that deciding to live one's life with another is an important act. And despite my fear, my despair at times, I retained the certainty that one day I would find love.

Love is a law of attraction.

If one's life is guided by the need for love, if one never
  forgets that it is life, then one day one will find it.
One other at least has this same desire.
For at least one other you are the irreplaceable person
  they are looking for.
And they are that for you.
But many fear to love.

Martha, of whom Dina talked to me in the evening when
the children were in bed, as we leaned on the wall of the
terrace looking at the distant town, the boats that with
luminously garlanded masts rode at anchor, Martha was lost
not only in the fear of being alone but in the fear of loving.

Love is passion.
Love is enthusiasm.
Love is risk.
Unloving and unloved, those who wish to spare,
  economize their feelings.
Love is generosity. Love is prodigality.
But love is exchange.
Who gives much receives much.
For we possess that which we give.

And sometimes a boldness is necessary. A sort of spon-
taneity akin to that of children.

Love is a virtue of childhood in the adult.

Martha—I listened to what Dina told me—had lost it. Or perhaps she had never known it. I looked at her. She took pains with her appearance, her hairdo. She would interrupt herself in mid-phrase to take out her compact, give her mirror a glance. She was closed in herself, too prudent for adventure to walk bareheaded in the wind.

"It would ruin my hairdo," she said. "I prefer staying here in the house."

Dina, Jack and I insisted. She refused.

"I went to the hairdresser's yesterday, Jack. You know very well we're invited to the Consulate tomorrow."

She was afraid of the wind, of the turbulence of love. Afraid of giving herself. How could she receive? Where was this fear from? Perhaps her education, a mediocre education that kills generosity, that brings the child up like a bookkeeper. That makes calculating people of men and women. "I will lend you this, but you lend me that." Bookkeepers looking for a profit.

To earn love you must first strip yourself, commit yourself. You must be ready to give all.

And no doubt she had not understood either that this law of love is also that of physical love. Doubtless she thought only of herself. And so closed in herself she was unable to receive. Unable to discover.

For loving understanding between bodies, each must

> *disarm itself and go toward the other, think of the
> other. Then it will find itself and find the other that
> finds it.*

But Martha thought above all of herself. Sometimes I
disagreed with Dina about her.

"You're unjust to her," Dina said. "She has lived only
for her children. She can't get used to the idea of not seeing
them any more. It's the opposite of egoism."

I differed. There are many ways of being egoistic.
Martha seemed to me to live only for herself. Her very love
for her children was possessive. I'd listened to her go on
and on about when her children were living with her.

"Now, they're no longer mine," she repeated.

> *But it is not love to hold another back. It is love to want
> the other to bloom, to follow the natural course of
> life.*
> *It is not love to mutilate and dominate another, but to
> accompany him on his way, help him.*
> *True love is the opposite of a wish for power.*

And Martha was avid, aggressive. I often saw her with
her lips clenched, eyes bright and staring as she seized
something, a fruit, or looked at Dina. In the glance she shot
Jack after dinner as he relaxed, unbuttoning his jacket and
stretching out his legs, I divined the anger that rose in her

simply because her husband seemed calm, relaxed, serene, happy. She rebelled, with a curt phrase:

"You certainly are relaxed." She hardly looked at him.

Dina laughed. "Leave Jack alone, Martha."

To know how to accept another as he is.
To be happy for him.
To love him in his totality such as he is, ugliness and beauty, defects and merits.
These are the conditions of love, of understanding.
For love is the virtue of indulgence, of forgiveness and respect for the other.

Perhaps it was too late for Martha. Too late for her to understand that she had been, that she was, her own and only executioner. She had condemned herself by a lack of audacity, of courage, to a marriage without love, and now by the accumulation of regrets and rancors, she had condemned herself to loneliness and bitterness. And yet even now she might have transformed her situation by intelligently accepting it.

There is only one way to live together.
There are a thousand roads that lead to happiness and peace.
Each may find his way when he endeavors to understand the other. And to understand the other we must see him, imagine ourself in his place.

*We must emerge from ourselves and our dreams. We
must see the real as it is.*

Tony nourished no illusions. When I knew him he was
living alone. He was one of the bricklayers I employed in
the construction of a villa that Dina had designed, an Italian
with a heavy, wrinkled face. A taciturn man of forty, he
worked from the crack of dawn, first in his garden and then
for me. He'd been divorced some years previously, his wife
having left him. I read the sadness in his eyes, in the sullen
energy with which he turned up the earth or stirred the
gravel or sand. Often Dina would ask him in for dinner. He
only smiled when he saw the children. His wife had taken
their only child, a little girl. And yet he was without resentment or hatred for her who had reduced him to solitude.

"What could I do?" he asked. "If she thought it was
better for her, I couldn't lock her in my house. You can't
force others to love you."

He saw his daughter once or twice a month. He was
happy in the days leading up to her visit, lapsing into silence when she left. Into his sadness without anger. His
daughter was well. That was enough for him.

*It is wisdom to know and admit to yourself that another
does not love you.*

That life continues despite the cruelty of this discovery.
It is wisdom to know that love is exchange; if the other
does not open to you, you will be closed to him.
The suffering will be double—in vain. Love is not born of
the lover's suffering. Perhaps pity—but pity is the op-
posite of love.

Tony understood this. He had accepted the choice of his wife, the separation, divorce and solitude. He was not happy, but he had the satisfaction of feeling that he had acted rightly.

Then day after day I felt that Tony was changing. He was more open, talked more. He accompanied me down the road to the workyard, leaned against a tree, commented on the work. I didn't ask, but I knew he was starting to see a young woman who'd moved into a little house on the edge of the forest. Months passed. They married. Then he decided to leave the area for a town on the coast.

"You understand," he said when he came to say good-bye, "this place is nothing to me, it's the past. Not that I want to forget it, but it will be easier to live with Emmanuelle elsewhere."

"Are you happy?" Dina asked.

Tony reflected. He was not a man to answer lightly.

"Happy? Yes, I think so. Not like before. It will not be like before. But you know, I never imagined it, but there are different ways of being happy. I think we are happy,

Emmanuelle and myself. She has had some unpleasant
experiences in life herself, and now we know how to begin
again."

For each couple there is a way that is theirs.
Each couple is unique. Because each being is unique,
in the encounter of two beings springs a unique
whole.
Each can find the other with whom he may begin or
begin again life together.

Each must invent love for himself. There can be no
model.
Each is king.
Each is an origin.

Tony did not forget us. He came back one or two times a
month for a surprise visit, sometimes alone, sometimes with
Emmanuelle. I looked at them, she who was not a very
beautiful woman leaning against Tony's shoulder as he
slowly spoke to her. Was she listening to him? I knew that
feeling when Dina spoke; I was not aware of what she said
but was enveloped in the gentleness of her voice. For Emmanuelle, it must be the same impression of peace and
calm, of equilibrium, of time that passed in tranquility. And
I knew that this feeling could rise only from the flowering
of the body and its feelings. In my life before Dina, I had
known many women. I spent many nights with them, many
months. Time in which to discover that we brought each

other nothing but a brief satisfaction, soon exhausted, that left us more alone than ever. Even my body, when I thought it was sated, I found to be restless, unsatisfied.

Man is not just a body.
Love is not just a meeting of two bodies.
To love is to share at the same time words, looks, hopes and fears. Those who mutilate love are forever ignorant of it. It is, indestructibly, made of the joy of bodies and the union of hopes. Indestructibly bound, like the branches of a tree that exists only in its roots.

One day, Tony and Emmanuelle stayed longer with us. It was, I remember so well, a winter dusk of mauve-colored skies over the sea. Our children were running ahead of us, toward Tony's little car.

"And you, what are you waiting for?" said Dina. "You must have children," she added with that resolute, almost authoritarian air she sometimes had.

"You see," said Emmanuelle, "Madame Gray says it too."

"Why don't you want a child, Tony?" Dina asked.

"I have a daughter, I know what it's like." He lowered his head.

"Problems, worries, and who can tell the future? I don't want to make that child's life miserable."

"And you, Emmanuelle, do you think of her?" asked Dina.

Emmanuelle stopped.

"It's not for myself, Madame Gray."

Tony had continued to walk ahead without looking around. I could see that he was listening like myself. Listening with his whole body.

"It's not for me, Madame Gray," Emmanuelle repeated, "it's for us, Tony and me. I am sure that a child would be good for both of us." She spoke with passion.

"I don't need one for myself, for myself alone, but I know that the two of us do."

What is a tree without its fruits?
What is love without plans, without a future?
And a baby is the natural future of a couple.
The face of the child is the face of the couple.
But sometimes a tree cannot bear fruit. Then other
plans are necessary. One must wish for another future
together. A future which the couple builds together is
the earth on which it stands straight, alive and one.

Dina and I had immediately wanted children. And I do not regret our having them despite the fate which overtook them, despite the wound which will never heal.

Life is a whole.
There is happiness, and there is unhappiness. Birth and
death.
To want one without the other is to refuse life.
To see only one or the other is to condemn yourself to
blindness and to multilate life.

I understood Emmanuelle, I supported her against Tony. I had experienced in myself the equilibrium that comes from having children. By their cries, their laughter, their running about, they affirmed the indefatigable project of their young lives stretched toward the future; they said that the future was before them and, thanks to them, before me.

I knew that at Treblinka and in the ghetto, for my father and other older comrades knew they were doomed, I represented the assurance that after them, despite the executioners, life would go on. For me, my sons and daughters were this vigorous image of the future. Now they no longer are, an amputation that I will always feel. I understood Emmanuelle.

Each of us needs to know that the future exists.
Each of us needs to leave some trace of his passage among men.
Each must wish to leave this mark. His mark. It is thus that humanity, a body with innumerable faces, ploughs its furrow.
And the child is the trace of a man and a woman.

But I also had friends for whom the trace was their work. There was Edward the sculptor, who recreated the world in his hands in tall forms of steel which he bent and folded.

"How do you do it?" I often asked him. "You and Liz, without children."

He shrugged his shoulders and laughed.

"You're a patriarch," he said. "You want to impose your
solution on me. A family. There is my family."

He pointed to his sculptures, the trees, the sky.

"Why imprison myself? My family is the world, images."

I was unconvinced. But I did not wish to disturb Edward and Liz if they were happy that way.

> *There are always many routes by which the stream can
> reach the sea.*
>
> *But the stream must go toward the sea and not lose itself
> in sands. A couple must be open to others. If not, they
> die.*
>
> *A couple must create–children or works or happiness for
> others. A couple must give their love.*
>
> *A love closed in on itself dries up and dies, like a plant
> without light. Children, works, the others, the
> world–that is the sun and the water by which love
> lives.*

Often with Dina, in the evening when the children were
in bed, I talked about love and the couples we knew. We
knew of so many failures—we ourselves, before we met,
had known bitterness and failure—that sometimes we had
the impression that we and our children were a kind of
exception. I loved to listen to Dina when she sat down at
the piano in the spacious music room. Now and then she

would interrupt herself to play a few notes. Then she'd take up the thread again.

"In the end," she said, "I think that Tony will accept. He wants a son as Emmanuelle does, but he is fearful."

"This divorce of Tony's," I said. "It was like cutting out part of his life. He suffered. That is why he's afraid now."

To divorce, to break one from the other, is always to cut yourself open. You must always be sure that the good derived from it will be greater than the suffering it entails.

Sometimes a tree, if too many of its branches are cut, will die.

And we must also think of the other, of others. Of all those whom the branches sheltered.

Dina played a few more notes, then stopped.

"But Emmanuelle will know how to give him confidence," she said. "She loves him, she wants to give him confidence."

To love is to give another confidence in himself.

Dina and I gave each other confidence. I understood so even more clearly when I heard Martha speak to Jack, when I saw how words can be a cancer between people. Martha was unaware of the harm she was doing Jack, of the harm

she did herself. She simply let herself be swayed by her
humor, the bitter satisfaction of giving pain. No doubt her
aggressiveness stemmed from a misery in herself. But she
did not know that one must want to make a couple for it to
come into being and flourish.

> *The harmony between two beings, their happiness, is
> also the fruit of their common will to build happiness
> and harmony.*
> *Love is not only the miracle born of an encounter; it is,
> day after day, that which they want it to be.*
> *You must decide to make it succeed.*

Where this will exists, it surmounts all obstacles. A couple of our friends lived a few miles to the east of les Barons, in
a beautiful Spanish-style house with a patio and fountains.
Americans. She had been a screen writer in Hollywood and
he, a vigorous man with white curly hair although he was
only forty, continued to write here his novels for young
adults. We were very fond of Barbara and David. They had
no children. Often they would visit us, to see and hear
Nicole, Charles, Richard, Suzanne.

Barbara smiled happily as she played with my children.
David stayed with me. We watched them.

"Barbara was made to have children," David said to me
one day. "And now this." He confided the fact to me objec-
tively, without bitterness. David had tried several doctors.
He had followed all the treatments, without success. Then,
he accepted. And Barbara also accepted.

"What was I to do?" he asked me. They tried to adopt a child but ran into various obstacles. They were waiting patiently, calmly.

"Barbara," said Dina, "now there's a woman, a real woman. She doesn't let it get to her. And yet I know she suffers."

Finally one day, when we blew the car horn as usual outside their house, David came running out toward us waving his hands.

"You'll see her waking up," he told us in a low voice.

Barbara was in the little room that looked out on the patio, where Nicole had often rested after running. Barbara was sitting by the bed. Lying on the covers curled up was a very dark-skinned Oriental baby. I looked at Barbara, who smiled at me. This little girl had a stump where a hand should have been. David took me outside.

"The war," he said. "She came from Vietnam. An orphan. She truly has nothing else. To us she can give something."

I don't know if I would have had the courage to endure minute after minute the spectacle of this mutilated arm. Of this foreign infant whom Barbara and David welcomed as their own daughter, who would become their daughter. In the months that followed I saw how Barbara bloomed, how David's laugh was stronger. How in giving their love Barbara and David had enriched their own. They had chosen to share with another who suffered. And they won. They had, even before adopting this injured baby, always participated in the world with enthusiasm, with indignation. Truly for

them mankind itself was their family. When I saw David, I
thought of my uncle Julek Feld who had been one of the
leaders of the uprising, one of those who did not think of his
own fate, his own mere life, but of the destiny of all. One of
those for whom ideals and generous ideas are the bread
they live by.

For my father, for Julek Feld, for David, loving meant
above all to be at the side of others, to fight for them, help
them, to defend and warn them from danger.

*To love is to feel that you are an active part of the
world. And responsible for yourself.*
To love is to understand that we live in others.
That you are a moment of the world.
*This love of the world, this love of the totality of life
allows us to fight death in ourselves.*
*To love the world, the others, is to abolish your own
death.*

DEATH

The telephone rang. I was alone in the room; outside it was raining, the damp wood fire was not drawing well. I was waiting for friends. The telephone, the voice of Bernard, terse. His son had had an accident driving along the sea.

"Don't come, Martin," he said. "But I wanted to tell you. He is dead."

I tried to speak, with difficulty as always at such moments.

"Don't come," he repeated. "I prefer to be alone."

He hung up. I hadn't known his son. Bernard didn't speak of him often. But I was stricken. All my wounds reopened at one blow.

Death is still with us, never abandons us.

I had encountered it in adolescence, in my city where war ravaged, where barbarism overran. Death became my everyday companion—death in the streets, heaped up corp-

ses, bodies that I'd buried in Treblinka under the yellow
sand. But my questioning then had nothing to do with
death. I was young, caught in the madness of war. My questions to myself were simple: "Why do they kill them? How
can I help them, revenge them?"

Years passed. One day, when I'd returned from Europe,
I met death once again. I saw my grandmother lying in her
bed in her New York apartment, small and stiff, wrapped in
her death clothes. I touched her cold forehead; I understood that she did not hear my crying, that she would never
again pass her hand through my hair to comb it for me. I
knew that I would never again feel her against me, frail yet
alive. Then for weeks I lived with the question burning
inside me.

Why death?

Life, my fate and others', seemed marred by injustice
because a day would come when we lost those we loved.

*Sooner or later the trial is there, in its insufferable
cruelty.*
Death, the unacceptable fact one must learn to accept.

I relived all my years at war, the days in the ghetto and
the terror of the nights in Treblinka.

Dina, my children, happiness—for a while, thanks to
them, I had kept death at a distance. But it returned, it took
them from me, and now it was prowling around me again.

Today, it was Bernard's son who was taken. I was stricken by his death because I know by all my suffering that the loss of a loved one is never erased.

We must know that death exists. We must know that it will strike all around us, in us, that which we love the most. We must not believe that we will be sheltered from this torment.
We must not forget it.
We must know that we will be wounded, that the wound will always live. And that we must nevertheless go on living.

I live. I am the proof that one can live through misfortune. And Bernard my friend will live also. Despite his grief. So it must be. But the question remains.

Why death? How do we live with it?

In Brussels one evening, as I was autographing my book *For Those I Loved,* a thin man with very dark hair tumbling over his forehead stayed by my side.

"I don't have any more books," I said, indicating the empty table.

"It's not that; I've already read, re-read it. I would like to talk with you. Will you?"

We went out. It was winter, damp, with a light mist. We walked in the nearly deserted streets.

"I am not a Jew, Mr. Gray," he began, "I am Catholic,

but your book for me was that of a believer. And yet you do not speak of God, you never mention His name. Only I know, I feel that you could not have survived in the midst of such barbarism, all those deaths, if you had not believed in God, in another life. How else could you have accepted the death of your loved ones? I lost my daughter, Mr. Gray. She was seven years old, an incurable disease. Do you understand me? I know that she lives in another way, like your children, and that we will find them again. Isn't that so, Mr. Gray? Isn't it?"

Another life after death?
A God, just and good, who gathers the souls of the dead?

So many times, without truly asking the question, I watched the religious Jews of the ghetto, those who accepted their own death as the price of fidelity to their moral law. So many times I had watched for a sign. For a long time I rejected faith, I committed myself to action—day after day to fight, to revenge.

Later, when I was sitting with Dina on the terrace at Barons, looking at the sky and sea, only later did I begin to think of God, to hear in myself that question, so simple, so naive, which nevertheless we hardly ever ask ourselves.

Why death, why life?

Leli, a gentle woman who came to help Dina, often prayed in a low voice. I used to smile at her for it and, perhaps without wishing to, with an air of mockery.

"Don't laugh, Mr. Gray," she said to me, "don't tease me. I'm sure He hears me. He sees us, He listens to us."

I would have liked to have such certainties. To believe in God would have given an order to the world. All the mysteries, all the outrages, the death of millions of men, and barbarism, good and evil, all would have been explained. Or justified, or comprehended in a larger mystery, that of the world, the universe. Then I lost Dina, my children. Everything became incomprehensible, chaotic, or was I truly meant to be struck down, punished, and for what?

The death of those we love, the death of children always seems unjust to us. A tree has been uprooted under which we loved to live, a tree is felled that had not yet given its fruit.

For some days I hated myself and the world. I was mad with sorrow, I shouted wildly all night, and when a few days later I saw Leli again, I wanted to cry to her, "Your God, now—you knew my children, you loved Dina, explain it to me. . . ." And then I began to act. My Foundation, the story of my life which I'd undertaken.

We escape the circle of death by action, by life.

I found myself in the same situation after escaping from the camp at Treblinka, when I wished to warn my own people of the fate that awaited them, to call them to arms. I recognized in myself this determination whose sources I did not clearly know but which was so deep—this instinct that had caused me to reject suicide in the barracks at Treblinka where so many of my comrades had let themselves be taken by death. I had resisted that temptation.

We must want to survive death. We must build by action, by thought barriers against despair.
The death of those you love is a cyclone that engulfs you, that you can allow to take you into oblivion. You must come out of the cyclone. You must wish to survive.

"I assure you, Mr. Gray, if I had not had this certainty that there is a God, if I had not believed, my wife and I would have let ourselves die. What was life without our little girl?"

The man in the Brussels street continued to talk to me. He left me no time even to try and answer him.

"It's as if I meet her everywhere, each thing, Mr. Gray, each child that I see tells me that she is no longer here. You understand?"

Then the man took me by the arm.

"I know, I should not tell you this. You too are like us. I have thought of killing myself, and my wife. But we are believers, we do not have the right. We will find her again, isn't it so? I am sure that she sees us."

We walked for a long moment in silence.

"Why don't you have another child?"

He shook his head.

"We don't have the courage. She is still so much there, we cannot replace her. And if fresh disaster befalls us? We're fearful."

"There is no other way," I said. "One must have this courage. That is what believing is, it seems to me."

To believe is to want to live.
To live to the end, despite death.
To believe is to believe in life.
To give life is to combat death.
Life must defeat death.
Each spring the tree flowers again. Autumn and winter
    are no more than seasons among the others.
Man must learn to see death as a moment of life.

"But you, Mr. Gray, what about you? Will you have other children after all that you've suffered?"

"If the time comes," I said.

One must not force the natural course of things.
There is a time for suffering and another for healing.

We walked silently awhile in the thickening fog.

"I would like to be sure," he said, "that I will find my daughter one day, that we will all three be together again, her mother, myself. I pray, Mr. Gray, I pray for it. I want to believe it."

I have never known how to pray. I have not learned to. I don't know if I should call myself a believer. But I am sure that I will never leave those I have loved. I live with their memory, and when death takes me I will close my eyes with them. Perhaps this is why I never answered clearly those who questioned me on my faith, on God, on another life, on what would come after death. I had but one certainty: those I had loved—all, those of the ghetto, my family, my comrades and then Dina and my children—live on in me. I felt that they still guided my steps. I had no need to call on their names, to pray for them. My life was theirs.

To be faithful to those who are dead is not to seclude yourself in sorrow.

We must continue to plough our furrow: straight and deep. As they would have done themselves. As you would have done with them. For them.

To be faithful to those who are dead is to live as they would have lived.

To make them live in us.

To transmit their face, their voice, their message to others.

To a son, a brother or to strangers, to others whoever they are.

And life cut short in those who have disappeared will thus germinate endlessly.

This was what I tried to explain in the streets of Brussels to that man I knew only by the sorrow he confided in me.

"But you are a believer," he said to me. "It doesn't matter what words you use, or refuse to. You are a believer. It is in everything you say. You believe in another life."

We arrived at my hotel.

"I would like to write to you," he said before leaving me. "I wanted to after reading your book, but was afraid to impose on you. Why should I bother you? You yourself have been struck by misery, and to speak to you of my grief, my daughter. . . ."

"If it helps you. But it is you who can do it all, you alone, from the beginning."

In ourselves, only in ourselves and by ourselves, we can decide to overcome the despair of death. But we must turn toward others. Toward life without number.
A tree survives first by its roots. But without sun it will perish.
Others are our sunlight.

It was already late. In the lobby of the Hotel Brussels two blond children, American no doubt, were sleeping in the same chair, their suitcases nearby. On the sofa, beneath a large tapestry, their mother was watching them with a smile. Life. A flash of memory, the nightmare of all those children I had seen dead, still warm, children I had laid in trenches at Treblinka, and then the little girl of the stranger and these two children, sleeping in the gentle looks of their mother. And millions of others, alive, joyous, like those who at Tanneron continued to run in the courtyard of the little school, in the village square. Mine were no longer with them. But the races, the games went on.

Since my tragedy I had often revisited the classrooms. I explained to the children the precautions to be taken against forest fires. I talked with the two teachers my children had loved.

I had feared this contact with the schoolmates of Nicole, Suzanne and Charles. Yet I did not leave the school in a mood of despair. There was a girl of ten or so who came up to me. Monique. I knew her parents, mimosa growers who had lost their flowered fields in the fire, that fragile wealth of small yellow gloves like little suns which before the fire had made the hill of Tanneron a golden sea.

"I remember them," Monique said. "Nicole best of all. She was my friend, you know, I won't forget her. Ever."

I embraced her. My children would live in Monique's memory.

One day, all the schoolchildren of Tanneron gathered on the highway leading into the town, where the car driven by Dina had gone out of control in the smoke and hurtled to the bottom of the ravine. With their teachers, they dedicated a stone marker. The wind played with their hair. I looked at their faces, so grave now, and I knew that they would not forget.

And the readers of *For Those I Loved* would not forget either—their letters told me so. Those I had lost would take up a new life in the lives of others. A multiple life. My children would live in Monique, in their schoolmates of Tanneron, in each of my readers, in those whom the Dina Gray Foundation warned of danger.

Was this not it, the other life, that which death cannot erase? The existence which can be eternal, which will endure as long as men endure and there is memory?

Man is mortal. The individual life ends one day. Those we love die. But children are always being born. There are people, life in countless faces that goes on and is amplified. The others, those who remain, those who are born, all mankind, preserve the memory of those who are dead. Death cannot be conquered except by fraternity with others.
I do not die because I am part of a living whole.

But this knowledge in no way takes from that wound which is the death of others.

Death is always the great trial.
The void that opens suddenly under our feet.
It is useless to flee it. We must learn to face it. And also to get around it.

In the months following the disappearance of my family,
I indulged in that void. For whole nights, in our big house
at Barons, I looked at the films which I had taken of them,
running in front of the house, playing with Dina.

I became mad, I lived with death. I wanted to submerge
myself in it, throw myself into its void as those who, seized
by vertigo, suddenly drop dead.

I regained my self-control. I thought again of the ghetto,
of Treblinka. I forced myself to look at death. I had forgotten it. Ten years of happiness, ten years of egotism perhaps,
ten years during which it had seemed that misery was no
more than a distant nightmare. Then it fell on me when I'd
lowered my shield. I remember a few months later I met
one of the doctors who had seen me at the time of the fire.
We were sitting on the terrace.

"You have recovered well," he said. "I was afraid for a
while; I didn't know then all that you had suffered already
in the war."

"And if you had known, Doctor, would it have reassured
or worried you?"

"There's no simple answer to that," he began.

He lit his pipe, bent forward, his fingers interlaced,
leaning his elbows on his knees.

"I am going to tell you a story as it was told to me. I
believe it to be true. There was a man in Israel who had
survived the death camps, a man who like yourself had had
to live with death, to handle the corpses of hundreds of
victims. He had managed to escape, he fought. Finally he

reached Israel. There he was married, but he did not wish to have children."

"Why?"

"I think he no longer believed in men. He was afraid of war. He did not wish to cast others than himself into that hell. I imagine that was more or less it."

"Do you think he was happy?"

"No, exactly. That is what I wanted to tell you. For years he had nightmares, constant insomnia. He went to see a psychiatrist, the friend who told me this story. The psychiatrist advised him to speak and write of what he had seen, the hell he had known in the camps. The survivor began doing so, and immediately improved. He slept. He even considered the possibility of children. He wrote for five or six months. Then he sent my friend the manuscript, and the same evening hanged himself."

The doctor tapped his pipe on the terrace wall.

"Perhaps I shouldn't have told you this."

I didn't answer. I imagined this unknown comrade who had relived his memories day after day. When, that last evening, he saw what he had recreated, it staggered him, as a mountain climber who has come too far and whose strength suddenly fails him at the precise moment he reaches the summit.

"That is why," the doctor went on, "I do not know what I would have thought if I'd known your past. Now I believe that your past, this barbarism you lived through, has helped you. You knew that death exists, you knew its face. Look

around you. Who, aside from those who like myself deal
with it professionally, dares to admit the presence of sick-
ness and death? How could you hope not to be prostrated
by them if you were unaware of them?"

> *Men today, society today, exclude, dissimulate misery
> and death.*
> *Which then strike us, unaware, like meteors.*
> *Misery and death are part of life. And man must learn to
> face them.*

"And you, Doctor? How do you react?"
"To what?"
"To death. You don't flee it, you can't flee it."
He replaced the tobacco in his pipe with slow gestures,
now and then looking at me over the top of his glasses.
"Don't you think we've talked enough about this?"
"I would like to know."
He remained silent a moment.
"I'll tell you about my first death. I understood everything that day. It was an old woman. She was already unconscious but seemed to be still suffering, breathing with
difficulty. Her daughter was sitting by her bed distraught.
I said to myself, 'What is the purpose of prolonging
this old woman's life? She is suffering, her daughter is suffering, and for God's sake why? At her age she doesn't have
a chance in a thousand of recovering.' I left after giving
some useless advice and medicine. Less than an hour later I

was called back. The sick woman had died. And then I saw, I understood. I had left a life, a rattling breath, nothing it seemed to me, and I returned to matter, stone, nothing. I understood that one must hold to life, prolong it to the end—even in atrocious suffering. For afterwards we do not know, but what I see before me is this body become like stone."

"You are not a believer?"

"Yes, I am."

The doctor got up and leaned on the wall of the terrace, looking at the sea. "It cannot be that all that which has been a man, a woman, is destroyed. I don't day this to mitigate your grief. I believe in my heart that a unique richness such as that of a man cannot become nothing. But I also know that it is necessary to preserve this richness. And for me the most noble commandment is the one which says "Thou shalt not kill.""

We must banish from the world all that may kill life. We must defend life from death.

And sometimes we must give death to protect men from those who are death's partisans, from systems that make death their instrument.

An idea is not great, a cause is not just unless the protection of life is at its heart.

"How do you avoid despair at this spectacle of death? How do you, doctor?"

"There are no miracles, believe me. It is always as bad
as the first time. I only know that this exists."

He indicated the sea, the golden sky, the trees, the
fields.

"The world, beauty—that, Mr. Gray, is my prime remedy."

*Against the anguish of death we must erect the bar-
ricade of life, we must realize the infinite beauty of
the world.*
We must lose ourselves in the mystery of the starry sky.
*We must become part of this great whole in perpetual
movement, part of the living universe.*

"And also . . . " he went on.

He showed me his surgeon's kit. ". . .this, action, struggle, not giving up to it. To try to wrest from it one second
more, a look, a breath. That is my other remedy. To act.
Ultimately I will lose, but it is in the nature of things and I
never surrender."

It is action and life that save us.

"And then hope. I am a believer, you know. This brings
me peace but there is something else, a sort of scientific
hope. I believe that one day we will live longer, that we
will attain a sort of equilibrium; we will have fuller lives

and death will be a term, a natural stopping place, a passage."

To consider death with open eyes. Because it is ineluctable.

Not to fear it, to give up to it.

To admit its existence and to fight it.

And to bring wisdom to bear when the moment comes.

When it strikes around us, those who have died continue to live in those who remain. They still live because the universe is an eternity that transforms itself.

And man is a particle of this universe, this eternity.

Like the universe, he transforms himself.

His death, that moment when life is shattered, is a passage.

For life in the universe never dies: it is eternal.

Death is no more than the end of one of life's forms.

Which are eternally reborn, in a million new forms.

LIFE

I had met Larry the first year we moved into les Barons. We were camping in one of the unfinished rooms. Dina was looking for a spring, and I had begun to clear away the undergrowth. Larry suddenly appeared late one afternoon. Dina and I were sitting against the stone wall of the house, warmed by the winter sun.

"Well, you're the Americans, as they say around here."

He spoke with a New York accent as he came forward, hands in the pockets of his leather jacket.

"Don't get up. I was passing through the village and they told me about you." He explained that he'd been living near Cannes for six years as a correspondent for one of the East Coast newspapers.

"I cover Europe," he went on.

Larry sat down facing us on a block of hollowed stone that must have been a trough.

"Everything okay?"

I was silent. I was already afraid of being invaded by the American population of the Côte d'Azur. Larry went on some more, then burst out laughing.

"You're not very talkative, I see. . . ."

He was still laughing as he got up.

"You know, when I came here I was looking for a quiet life. I wanted to see only the neighbors I wanted to—no intrusions, nobody coming to tell you that they worked for a newspaper in Boston or Los Angeles."

His laugh was contagious. We stood up.

"That's just how it is," I said. "When one comes here from New York, one wants a little peace."

"And not to meet someone from New York."

He rubbed his hands.

"You're adorable. I tell you, you won't see me again, but to know you're around enchants me. So long." We accompanied him to the gate.

"Life is amusing, joyous. I love it, life, chance encounters. That's why I like my job. There's always something to discover, you, this. . . ."

Larry gestured toward the sea horizon, the banks of dark clouds fraying in the wind.

"Beautiful, isn't it?"

He laughed silently.

"And this fresh air—you smell the pines? It's beautiful, life. I remember . . . do you have a moment?"

Larry had conquered us. I felt an almost involuntary smile come to my face. I saw Dina was smiling also.

"Good, all I really have to tell you is this: one evening in Korea after a battle, two or three trucks were still in flames, the dead were being carried away, the wounded . . . I was there, sitting on a hillock with this. . . ."

Larry touched his leg, lifted the cuff of his trousers. There was a long red scar on the calf.

"It was a nasty wound. I was thinking they'd have to amputate, when. . . . There was a river and the sun was behind something, I don't know what, when by a strange trick of light it made the river shine. I was tired, wounded, my leg, these soldiers dead for nothing or not much, and then suddenly this light, this river, this calm. I felt joyous, drunk with joy. I told myself that despite everything life was beautiful, strong, great, beautiful and that I loved it, a little like this evening. You understand? Peace."

He went off limping, waving back to us, revving the motor of his car.

"Till next time, Larry," cried Dina.

That night we went walking on the deserted road. We were learning the landscape which was to be our surroundings; we listened to the wind, the silence. I remembered that night when I'd jumped from the train, the night I escaped from Treblinka, when I felt the earth, water and grass under my palms and then marched through the forest and slept there. I had just left the unthinkable hell of men and yet, not merely because I'd made my escape, I like the wounded Larry had experienced the conviction that life was beautiful despite all, despite the yellow sand of Treblinka.

I pressed Dina's shoulder. She let herself go against me.
"What is it?" she asked me.
"Life, I love life."
Dina stopped. Through the trees one could see the
town, its lights coming on in the gathering darkness. The
harbor lights were reflected on the somber expanse of the
sea.
"It's beautiful," Dina murmured.
Then she embraced me.
"It's life which is beautiful," she added.

*Life, life changeable as the sky, clear then stormy,
generous life like the rains of spring, life savage and
cruel as the hurricane, life which takes away and re-
turns manifold, life . . . one must learn to love and to
realize its beauty, its clearings within the storm, its
breadth and majesty, because it is man and the universe.*

Several times after my tragedy, I had come down this
road where Dina and I had walked those first evenings. I
relived those moments, I saw the lights of the town again.
And I dared to say again, "I love life." Larry had become a
frequent guest at Barons. The children would play with
him, and he always had a story to tell them—they ran after
him as he fled laughing and limping.
    After the fire, he was one of the first to visit me, to
dare—so many of my friends were afraid—to confront my

sorrow. It was about a week after the tragedy. Was I alone? Suddenly I felt a hand around my neck, a warm hand. I turned around. It was Larry. I learned later that he had come from Germany. As soon as he heard he had left his work, he was there, silent, red-eyed. We wept on each other's shoulders.

Then we sat down across from each other. I believe the night passed. Now and then Larry would speak, but it was only to make me speak, tell of my past. Suddenly the barriers in myself were down, barriers which had held back my memories of the ghetto, of the war, of all the corpses I had handled bodily at Treblinka, of the conflagrations I had seen, of the burning ghetto, of the cement that had burned, and now of the forest that had burned.

"You don't know, Larry. I will tell you." I believe that is how I started, and I did not stop until I'd run through it all, from the war to the death of Dina and the children. Then I fell into a brief exhausted sleep from the effort of having relived it all. Oblivion. When I awoke, Larry was there.

"I have faith in you," he said. "I have faith in you, Martin. You will go on living."

He clenched his fists.

"It's another blow, Martin, a blow that has cut you in two. But it is life just the same, and you will live through it."

He got up, limping back and forth in the room Dina had designed.

"You have died again for those you loved, but you will be reborn. It's the law of life. We must respect it."

Life's pendulum swings between darkness and light, despair and hope, torment and peace.
Life has always to be reconquered.
Those who believe that they have achieved the last obstacle are mistaken: there is always another obstacle.
Another battle.
When struggle ends, when an unfeatured plain stretches before you, with no walls to impede progress, that is the time of death.
To be born is by definition to struggle, to suffer, to be torn from the passive, warm sweetness of the breast. We must accept suffering and strife. They are life.

For several days, Larry did not leave my side. He was there, active, speaking only when he sensed I craved for a voice to stifle the voices of despair that howled inside me. It was during those days that he told me the story of his father, a woodcutter who had slowly made his fortune until he'd become a lumber dealer, a force of nature, a giant with a mighty laugh, who each morning would go out into the woods to inspect the cuttings and oversee his workers. Then one morning, when he was about sixty years of age, he was unable to get up.

"The spinal column," said Larry, " a kind of paralysis."

It was several weeks before he could walk again with the aid of a cane.

"He was never able to accept it."

He became violent, he hurled his cane against mirrors, windows. He shouted with rage.

"He took it out on me," Larry said. "He said I was nothing but a pencil-pusher, incapable of replacing him. That was when I left. My father died soon afterward. Why am I telling you this now?"

We were walking through the charred trees, crushing trunks that dissolved in ashes under our feet.

"Why? Because I have often thought of my father, for years. With remorse, also in an attempt to understand what he felt. And there was my leg wound, the fact that I could not walk as before, an accident that brought me close to my father. I believe I actually realized what he must have felt, and how I must live, or try to. That is why I am telling you, Martin. My father," Larry continued, "found himself brutally confronted by his old age. It had been nothing but a word for him, and suddenly he could no longer walk. He had had no time to adapt himself. He wasn't ready. You have to accept, Martin, to get over it better. In our life there are beings who are a part of ourselves, who disappear taking that part with them. And yet one must go on, start over. Accept death, old age."

Like the sun, life describes a curve. One day it begins to decline, slowly. We must prepare for this time, accept it. To know that this second half of life is also life. That it can be as full as the first half.

There are twilights that are more beautiful than dawns.
We must simply wish them to be.
And illuminate others and ourselves by our inner peace.

"Accept?"

I revolted against the idea. And if I'd accepted as much as I could, what if one day a man feels that he cannot find the road again?

"You're unfair, Martin, unfair to life."

I shouted, grabbed Larry by the arm and shook him. I told him about my children, Dina and my family in the ghetto.

"You can't know all of your life yet," Larry said. "It is full, overflowing, but you know only a part of it. It continues despite everything, and so must you."

We resumed our walk in silence.

Why did certain faces come back to me? Why? No doubt because of Larry's words: I thought of Rivka, the young girl I'd known in the ghetto. Rivka taken off to die, and so many others. My lacerations were, after all, life and I could continue to act, to have my effect on it.

"What do you think of this foundation against the destruction of nature?" I asked Larry.

He put his hand on my shoulder.

"That's it," he said. "That is the road you must take."

Life is above all a project, projects that we must set for
ourselves.

146

What is important is that it inscribes itself in the real world.

Action is real life.

Life is constructing, building, raising up. Stone after stone, thought after thought, act after act, to study ourselves and the world in order to know one's self and it, to change ourselves and change the world.

To achieve inner peace, which alone endures.

To make the life of man less cruel.

To hold out the hand, the voice, the look to those who call out.

A few days later I left for Paris. I tried to carry out my project. The people I met there helped me to go on. Not because they distracted me from my suffering. That was in myself. But because they forced me to reflect on myself, and on life. On what had happened to me. And then there were those who helped me because they needed me. They compelled me to transcend myself, discover in stating the ideas I had not known were mine, which came to me thanks to them.

You must give yourself projects that enlarge you. That bring your highest energies into play.

That oblige you to choose the peak rather than the ditch.

Generous projects that make your life generous.

And that give free play to the life of man, by which it ennobles itself.

147

I had been in the habit, when I arrived in Paris with
Dina, of going to a hotel on one of the great boulevards. I
knew that I shouldn't but I went back there after my
tragedy. There was a new concierge, a youngish man who
recognized me from my picture in the papers. They'd carried articles on the Dina Gray Foundation, on my tragedy.
When I came back late at night I'd sometimes stop by his
office, reluctant to be alone.

"If I'd been you I would have attacked the government,
found out who was responsible," he said to me. Hundreds
of other people had told me this. But how would this legal
action have helped me in a larger way? I was discovering
rules that we must observe if we are to act and come into a
larger life.

> *One does not construct against something or someone.*
> *A life, if one wishes it to be full, must not be built*
> *against but for something or someone.*
> *For.*
> *Because a life is a totality, a single plant. And if we claw*
> *at others, we claw ourselves within.*

In this manner I got through the first months. And by
action, thanks to others, I came alive through them.

> *Life is a tree that the storm buffets. We must hold our*
> *branches intact, we must wish to remain rooted in place*
> *until the wind, the storm, die down.*
> *If they ever die down.*

A few miles from les Barons, in a small town by the sea, lived a happily married couple. He was a small, thin man of Italian origin who gestured as he talked; she was a tall woman from eastern France, blonde and delicately built. Whenever I met them they were hand-in-hand. As they walked toward me they communicated their happiness to me. Françoise had been married once before, unhappily. Back from Paris, I sat down at their great hearth.

"Well, how is it going, your foundation?" Louis asked. "Can I get you something to drink?"

They enveloped and warmed me with their affection. Françoise accompanied me out.

"What can I do, Martin? Tell me. I'm ashamed to be so happy with Louis, with all this unhappiness around us."

She answered the letters that came to the Foundation. She devoted herself to her work. One day, in my Paris office, I found her sitting by herself. It was several weeks since I'd been back to les Barons. Françoise had lost weight, her eyes were red. I closed the door.

"Louis," she began. "The doctors are not sure. It may be cancer. They don't give me much hope."

In her life, in their life, a chasm had suddenly opened beneath their feet. The ground that had seemed solid, like that I had hoped to build my happiness on, had suddenly crumbled to nothingness.

"Not much hope," she repeated. "Martin, what am I to do?"

I looked at her. I was speechless. All my misery, my

despair which I'd begun to contain, overflowed, submerged me.

> *In life, nothing is ever finally resolved.*
> *One must always be on guard. Ready for the sudden squall. Capable of seizing the beauty of an evening, of a morning, of an instant. For the next day, the next day can be swept away in torment.*

"Come," I said. "You have to get out of here. Let's take a walk."

I was the one who needed air and light to reassure myself, needed to see people in the streets apparently happy, to give myself confidence again.

> *We must not let ourselves be contaminated and destroyed by misery. We must fight against it, not feed it with shared tears.*
> *The man who suffers and fears needs not another cry of grief, but a voice stronger than his that lends him strength.*
> *To fight the fire is not to prolong it or kneel before it so that it consumes us.*

Outside on the Champs Élysées the sun was shining brightly and a keen winter wind was blowing.

"He is still alive," I said to her. "You must save him, you mustn't show him this face, you must have confidence."

First, to drive out fear. To restore inner calm, to tell
yourself that there is always another chance.
That all the world's happiness is possible while life ex-
ists.

"Nothing is certain," I repeated. "Nothing. And even if
it were, he must be kept alive until a treatment is found.
You must try everything, Françoise. Everything, and you
must protect him from despair." We were walking quickly,
I was making Françoise keep up with me. The cold
weather, action had bit by bit restored my courage. I talked,
I looked at the clear sky. I remembered my father: You must
seize the chance, Martin, he always said, the first chance.
But to have this attitude it was necessary to believe that
there was a chance, always.

To live is not merely to let yourself go with the stream.
One day, the current will no longer bear you. One
day, the whirlpool will take you under, into a
morass.
To live is to know why you live.
To live is to wish to live.
To live is to have faith in life.

Françoise suddenly stopped me.
"Enough, Martin, enough."
She looked fatigued, weary.
"I know that he doesn't have a chance, I feel it, I tell you

that I feel it. What is the use of making him suffer, of making myself suffer?"

The resolute tone of these words reached me, pierced
me. I avoided her eyes, looking away to draw strength from
the bright sky, the faces of unknown passersby. I mustn't let
her take me under like those drowning swimmers who take
their rescuers down with them. I took her by both arms.

"Don't say so, don't say so. You cannot, you must not
think this for even a second. Don't say it."

Thought may be a seed of life or of death.
It must be a seed of life.
You must fight with yourself, grow above the black
thoughts that invade the spirit like a clinging fog.
Thought must be a support of life, a source. You must
wish to germinate clear thoughts.
And if you are unable to, if the strength is lacking for a
time, then you must refuse to think, numb yourself
with sounds and images, actions and voices. You must
help yourself to live. And sometimes have the courage
to flee.
Thought must not become a venom.
You must not deny life in either word or thought.

I took Françoise back to her hotel. We had said little
since that moment. I held her arm, I tried to give her courage, to make her feel that I was with her. Not merely because I had no more to say, but because I experienced her
disquiet myself.

Life is sharing. Not to remain shut up in one's self.
It is to open your life to the world.

"Martin," she said as she left me, "I will do what I have
to. I am going to pray. I know how to be strong."

I saw them frequently after that. Louis moving with difficulty but smiling. Françoise by his side. She held his
hand, and spoke as gaily as if the sun were not hidden, as if
the road before them had always been straight. The doctors
came. One of them I knew well confided in me one day.

"She is extraordinary," he said. "I didn't think her capable of such self-control."

Françoise had not imagined either that she would be
capable of it.

We never believe enough in ourselves.
We are forever ignorant of the resources of life.
But life is to dare to break through the walls that we
*   erect before ourselves.*
To transcend the limits we impose on ourselves.
Life is always to go beyond.

I could have told the doctor so many stories of the men,
women and children the war forced to go beyond themselves, who had resisted torture, fatigue, hunger and fear.
Innumerable heroes. Simple people. Sometimes I had been
tempted to evoke for Nicole, my eldest daughter, some of
these episodes. The children of the ghetto younger than
myself, who ran from roof to roof, ruin to ruin, with mes-

sages or arms. Then I would look at Nicole, I would measure her calm happiness. Why speak to her of that now? The
time would come.

The time will not come.

I still have my memories. But they help me. He helps
me and teaches me, that man who near death found the
strength to rescue a child trapped in a burning street.
Where had he found such strength? Bleeding and enfee-
bled by months of near starvation, where but in his spirit?

> *Spirit, will and thought can multiply the forces of life.*
> *For them to be able to, one must wish it so.*
> *It is the invisible power of will and thought that permits*
>   *us to seize life in both hands.*
> *And that is why we must be attentive to our thought:*
>   *live by it, and live by the spirit. For we cannot live*
>   *long against our thought without damage to ourselves.*
> *If we do so, it will be a barrier. Like the scorpion's sting*
>   *it can be an invincible weapon or turn on itself.*
> *To know it, to master it, to respect and utilize it is the*
>   *great adventure of life.*

The doctor was speaking. Of the chances of survival for
Louis, even for Françoise.

"She's beginning to smile," he said. "Believe me, that's
not easy."

Then he caught himself.

"But of course, you know how hard it is."

Silent a moment, he lit his pipe.

"I believe she prays a great deal. It helps her."

Had I ever prayed? I had never had time to learn real prayers, the ordered words men employ when they address God. Had I had the time even to think of God in my young life deranged by war and later in my struggles in the United States? But I had seen believers kill men, turn them over to the barbarians. I had seen believers, Christian and Jewish, lose faith. And I had known men without religion who gave their lives for others and who kept their faith. One day, they said, there will be a just society. That is why I had not attached much importance to prayers learned by heart, to faith in an official God.

There was a right way in life for whatever reasons one followed it, and there were sinuous ways, the paths of egoism and betrayal, which were none the better for being disguised in finely worded proclamations of lofty intentions and fidelity to God.

Acts make and judge a life.
Not words. Not intentions.
But a word or thought can provoke an act or prevent it.
  One must be careful with one's thoughts and words.
  They are cancer or energy.
They disintegrate or bring together.
A word, a thought in a life can be an act.

I often went to see Françoise and Louis. He was sitting

in an armchair before a window with a view of the port. He remained seated. Françoise smiled.

"He is better," she said.

Her voice was assured, there was certainty in her voice.

"I am grateful for this experience. We know even better now how much we love each other."

She laughed. I made myself laugh with her. She was a different person. Before Louis's illness, Françoise had often irritated me with her conventionality. She played at being a woman of the world. When Dina and I visited her she would try to astonish us with her chic. What saved her from being ridiculous was the love she gave and received from Louis. Her devotion also to me after the fire and Dina's death had revealed in her something else besides the appearance of fine and beautiful attitudes: true feelings.

Now I really discovered her. Courageous. Dignified. Tranquil and true. As if misery and ordeal had stripped away the decor to reveal the noble framework of her personality.

She reminded me of a Polish peasant woman, a nondescript woman, tough and taciturn. Or so she seemed to me at first. I'd known her when I'd gone back to Warsaw. She sold me some bread, as if reluctant to. I wanted to talk to her as she stood in her doorway. To move her, to ask her for help.

I remember her round face and gray eyes, the child clinging to her long, black pleated skirt, the cross she wore, the rapid gesture with which she took my money. I was in rags, covered with mud. I must have looked feverish. She'd taken the money and shoved me away to close her door. I left, sad and angry, judging this woman harshly, condemning her indifference and egoism. Several months later I encountered her in a forest, fighting for the resistance, transformed. The Germans had burned her village. She no longer knew where her husband and child were. She was here. Upright. I recognized her gray eyes. I had a few words with her. She didn't remember me, but said:

"I must not have helped you much. I didn't know, I knew nothing. But I have learned. I ask you to forgive me for that time."

Crossing herself, she added, "I will pray for you."

Then she left to rejoin her comrades, upright and dignified.

Personal misfortune had opened her to the world.

And there had been all the others. Those forced to live in the ghetto, who in two or three weeks had gone from peace and wealth to hell and starvation. Their masks fell away then, and revealed who they truly were. Some became beasts of prey, killing for a piece of bread, turning in their parents for an added day of survival. Others, who before may have been criminals, became heroes sacrificing their lives.

Ordeal, as for Françoise, forced them to reveal their true faces.

Ordeal is the moment that tests the truth of a life.
Before it, you never know everything about a man.
Then comes the storm: trees fall, some which you
thought strong buckle and capitulate, others thought
to be cowards stand up and fight.
The ordeal is merciless. It allows us to know others and
ourselves. Those who are nothing fall apart even if
they have built a face of marble.
And in every life there is an ordeal.

Sometimes we walked, Françoise and I, along the
promenade by the sea. We didn't speak of Louis, nor did I
mention my own lost loved ones. We had to face ourselves,
each in our way.

To turn ourselves toward the future. Françoise was inspired by her hope, the war that she waged against illness.

"I try to live in the present," she said. "If I think of all
we hoped for, it would only be a matter of months." And
myself? And them, those people herded into the death
camps. I quickly distinguished, after a day—so long, a day
in Treblinka—those who would manage to survive awhile.

They faced the present. They did not turn back to what
had been their lives.

Others, on the contrary—and not only the old—who had
escaped the first executions, had expressionless eyes. They
were not facing the present, they did not try to seize the
slim chance which would perhaps be offered them. They

were living in the past. Perhaps at Treblinka this was an answer, a way of fleeing into death from its hell.

But I had encountered this malady in other places as well. In New York I had known a young woman, an antique dealer, who had a shop near mine on Third Avenue which had belonged to her parents. Jenny had gone into the business with them. Then they died. This is a law of life itself, but Jenny refused to admit it.

I visited her shop to offer some suggestions. I found her sitting in the back, her elbows propped on a marquetry table, her chin in her hands. I recognized those inexpressive eyes focused on the past. We talked. I went back to see her. I found her beautiful and sad. I thought it was vain, even shameful, to let one's life go to seed in contemplation of a past which could not return. I tried to bring her out of it, to take her with me on one of my trips to Europe. Jenny shook her head.

"No, really, what good is it? You know I'm not interested in much. Why all the fuss?"

I found her beautiful; I hoped to form a relationship with her which would be a source of pleasure to us both. I insisted.

"No, Martin, I have to visit my sister in Oregon. I prefer to," she answered.

She did not wish to extricate herself from the swamp of memories. Her father, her mother, her sister—she loved them. Who doesn't love his family? But her parents were dead, and the sister was married. Why then?

"Come out of it!" I was angry with her. But I hurtled

against that passive gaze which denied life. One day the
store did not open. Jenny had left for Oregon. She never
returned to New York.

Buried under her memories.
It is not to the past that our lives must turn but the
future.
For life is a river that flows into the future and cannot
be stemmed.
That is why tomorrow must be more important than
yesterday.
To cling to the past is to be caught in a Sargasso Sea that
paralyzes, kills our courage to live.
And we drown in it.
We must stay in the middle of the current. We must
know that today is born of yesterday and flows into
tomorrow.
We must go with the current of life: yesterday has been,
there are our roots, but the fruits of the tree ripen
today and will be harvested tomorrow.

I felt all this in myself when I went back to the hotel in
Paris where I had lived with Dina. I went there but I was
wrong, as Jenny was, to constantly confront myself with the
vanished past, wrong to imagine that that was fidelity to my
loved ones.

In fact, I was recoiling on myself like a sick plant.

I spent the night open-eyed in the noisy hotel room. The

past returned in waves, it smothered me. To escape it, I turned on the radio. In vain, because this room was of that past. One night, unable to bear it any longer, I went out and walked along the boulevards. I believe that it was on this night that I decided never to forget Dina and our children, but never to allow myself to be overwelmed by the despair of having lost them. On the contrary, I had to go forward. To live a new life.

To change, to begin again is not to deny one's self but to transcend one's self.

A few days later, Louis died. I returned to les Barons as soon as I could. I went down to the little town by the sea where they lived.

Françoise was home, in a house that seemed also to have died. I forced her to leave the room where she had lived by Louis's side these past months. She let me, gently weeping. I took her to Paris to stay with friends. We saw each other again after some time had passed. Time effaces nothing but it forces one to admit that the loved one will not return. That his death is not a nightmare which will dissolve with a new morning. Françoise and I had a calm talk. Each in control of his grief, accepting life as it was.

"What are you going to do?" I asked.

"What do you mean by that?" Françoise answered. She smiled at my astonishment.

"I no longer want to live shut up in myself," she con-

tinued. "You know, during these last months, taking care of
Louis, I believe I have learned a great deal about him,
about myself and about you. Louis and I were living like
plants in a hothouse. True, we loved each other, but what
did we know of others and the world. We were closed in on
ourselves, Martin, and perhaps you and Dina also, your
children, were sealed off in your happiness. I don't want to
live shut up in misery. I want to get out of it, Martin."

She took my hand.

"I am going to try," she added.

It was Françoise who taught me a lesson. I looked at
her; she'd become another person, courageous and resolute.

Life: each of us makes it a new, personal experience.
And from all experience, sweet or harsh, we must ex-
tract some good.
There is no event without its meaning for a life.
Not a day, not a trial but has its significance.
On condition that we do not contemplate them, fasci-
nated and immobilized like a serpent's prey, but use
them as a help in going forward.

Toward what?

I had often asked myself this question. In the war it had
been vengeance; Berlin had been my goal. Then in the
United States I'd aimed at success and happiness.

Now, what is my goal? Mine, and others'?

"To get out of yourself, Françoise—what does that mean for you?"

"First of all, it means not giving up. It seems to me that I've reached an equilibrium. On one hand, there is a sort of abyss. And sometimes I want to fall into it. On the other hand, I do not know what there is. But I know that life is there. So I cling to that, I try to move away from the other."

In each life there comes a moment when an abyss opens up before, by and inside one's self. To live is to succeed in not falling into it. To live is to know how to confront it and leave it.

To live is to advance: to grow, to open out toward happiness but to know how to learn from unhappiness.

To make of dry periods and times of storm the means to strengthen and test ourselves. To raise ourselves, not in relation to others but ourselves.

To live is to expand. To become fully what one can be.

After that, I did not see Françoise. I learned later that she took a course in nursing and left with a medical relief mission for Asia. My friend the doctor, who reported this to me, added:

"It's a flight. Not very sound psychologically—a form of suicide but better in the end, one she'll recover from."

"And me, doctor—what am I fleeing? And you?"

My tone was angry. Did he understand that his reaction

was that of one who admits only one way of life, the individualist, the egotist, and that there were other ways which sometimes appeared far-fetched but might be more generous?

"If she wanted her life to have a direction, a new one. . . ."

The doctor got up.

"Perhaps," he said, "if it corresponds to something profound in her, but if it is no more than a superficial whim which she has given in to, if she's giving up what counts for her. . . ."

"One must wait, doctor. I hope, I believe she has found what matters to her."

To live is to know what counts in your life. What you place the highest. To reestablish the order of importances. It is different for each. We must find our own. Not to imitate that of others. To create our own way. And to be convinced of its rightness. The life that we have refused to live, the life which was in us and which we stifled, grows day by day into a destructive force that like a rising tide undermines the personality, destroys all possible happiness. Buries the future under the regrets of a missed life.

Françoise found her way. I know that now that I have seen her again, thinner but rejuvenated. She came to the office of the Foundation in Paris on her first return to Europe. It was she who questioned me.

164

"Martin, how is it going for you?" She was concerned for the Foundation. "It's important, Martin, you've created something. You must go on."

I looked at her with astonishment. "And how are you?"

She was silent a moment.

"I've learned a great deal out there."

She smiled.

"More. I had already learned from the illness and death of Louis. I have found a new way to live, one I believe suited to me."

She explained to me the work her group did, the misery of the refugees. She spoke calmly, as if she had achieved a sort of fullness, a peace.

To live is to create your own world. To find your peace. And for each it is different. It can come out of misery if you transcend it. Each can achieve it. But you must wish to. And to know that peace will come only when you form relationships with others. Family or group, bonds of speech or thought—it hardly matters. But they are necessary.

There is no fullness if you are a solitary tree. It is the forest that gives its meaning to the tree and makes it vigorous.

I was happy for Françoise's victory. I went home, to a place outside Paris since I'd decided to leave the hotel where the past was stifling me. There I had a garden, some trees. Silence, and occasionally the sound of the wind.

I stretched out on the grass. The sky was not that of
Provence. Full of clouds, here, variations. Clouds and clearings. Like life. Children were running their rulers along the
grill of the fence. I heard their voices, laughing and teasing
each other. They were life in its future power, in its joy.

*To live is to be in the world with joy. It is to wish for this
joy, to retain it. To refuse to be overrun by the gray
weeds of sadness. To live is to commit one's self to
action. To live is to be one's self. It is to resist and to
love. To accept and refuse.*
To live is to create.

THE
ABYSS

I had known Marc for several months. He was dark-complexioned, thin, with a hatchet face. He was often taken for a Spaniard with his very dark hair and thick, lusterless skin.

I had employed him to work with me at the Foundation. He had connections in press and publicity circles, and since I was about to approach the public and the government I needed the help of journalists.

One day, shortly after the publication of *For Those I Loved*, he entered my office with a folder full of articles on the book and the disaster which had befallen me. He opened it in front of me—all headlines, big photographs.

"It's extraordinary, isn't it?" Marc began. "Now you are famous, you're known everywhere."

It even happened that people would stop me in the street. I'd appeared several times on television, and that seemed to give people the right to talk to me about my family, to bring up their own problems and offer me their support. At first I was irritated by this, tormented like an

animal driven from cover. But behind the slightly morbid
curiosity I discerned most often a sympathy. I accepted it. If
I wanted to bear witness, to reach the public, I would have
to play the game.

"You're famous," Marc repeated. "It's come overnight,
do you realize that? Writers and moviestars have never had
so much written about them."

He took out the largest-circulation evening paper in
Paris, and showed me a full spread devoted to what were
described as my adventures.

"Fame," Marc concluded.

He spoke with the unconsciousness of a young man who
has never known sorrow. No doubt he noticed that I did not
share in his enthusiasm. He closed the dossier and left.

Fame? Being known? I had paid for this with blood.
How could Marc imagine that these pages, these scraps of
paper impregnated with ink that one called newspapers,
how could he believe that this material could make me
happy for a moment? Of course, I had done what was
necessary for my book to become known. And the journalists had helped me with their friendship and understanding.

But the desire for fame, notoriety, was an abyss into
which I never risked falling.

And not merely because of my misfortune, but I had
discovered that fame was a bottomless gulf, a mirage. When
I fought with the Soviet Army—just before our entry into
Berlin when I was decorated with my comrades in the pres-

ence of our unit—I understood then that distinguishing myself was no alcohol that inspired me. I often think of Boris, a blond curly-haired boy who was transformed by this decoration. I felt that the red star on his chest did away with the man he had been. He stuck his chin out, threw back his shoulders.

"You understand," he said to me, "we are no longer officers like the others."

He spoke vehemently. He no longer drank with the men. Often he threatened them. When we entered the outskirts of Berlin and fought skirmishes in the ruins, he recklessly exposed himself but also ordered his men to fight in the open. He wanted to be the first, and it was the men killed under him who made him a hero. He thought he had what he wanted.

> *But those who make fame and the opinion of others their life's goal are always panting after it like a thirsty dog. They never find peace. Glory and others' opinion of one's self are as changeable as the clouds of a stormy sky.*

I kept away from Boris. He was lost, he craved the hypocritical, servile look of admiring complicity from others as an addict craved his daily dose. He would do anything for it. I learned later that he'd entered the Russian security police immediately after the war. He must have become one of those police who arrested and accused inno-

cent people. To assure their own promotion, their fame and
rise in rank.

*The search for glory, ambition, the taste for power and
authority are like wounds that open, gnawing diseases
that slowly destroy the personality.*
*For the equilibrium of a life must be established within
ourselves. By ourselves. All the rest is fragile, uncer-
tain, transient.*
*Fame and ambition (when it is not the desire to become
a better person) are gangrenes. Diseases of men, abysses into which they fall.*

In New York, Dina introduced me to Jane, a young
woman who laughed a little too loud and too often for my
taste. She was a model as Dina had been, and went through
many lovers, discarding the head of a fashion house for an
editor-in-chief. And it worked. Her photographs flooded
the magazines. Sometimes she took a screen role. She was
promised a sensational debut in a musical comedy.

One night we all went for dinner to a Chinese restaurant
on Broadway. Jane was laughing hysterically. She opened a
magazine on the table.

"Dina, look. Martin, you don't know what this means in
the business." It was a double page in color. Jane was reclining half-nude on a white fur covering. Jane, with bare
breasts.

"You're not jealous because Martin is seeing this?" she asked Dina with a laugh.

I was silent. It was during the course of such evenings that I decided to leave New York, to live far from the city, in a place where Dina and I, in our new life, would choose our friends, would escape—and above all, the children we would have—this world of false values.

Jane talked a lot that evening. Her projects, her rise to fame which was beginning. So rapid and exciting, as she said. Occasionally Dina, in a voice in which I felt a sort of growing terror, would interrupt Jane's nonstop discourse.

"Jane, are you sure? If all this doesn't work out you're going to be terribly disappointed. Take care. Everything is going well now, Harold wants to marry you. You don't think you should. . . ."

Jane laughed again. Harold was a talented publicity designer who despite Jane's vagaries continued to love her, to propose marriage and a new life to her.

"Harold—are you kidding, Dina? My career would be over. He wants to smother me under roses of love, love, but he'll smother me."

We accompanied Jane back to her place. She insisted we come up for a nightcap.

We went upstairs. She had a small apartment full of big photographs of herself. On the tables and the bed were piles of magazines. She spoke with sweeping gestures, pointed at the photographs.

"You remember, Dina? You were still with us then. It was ... don't say, I don't want to know. Time goes so quickly." She suddenly became somber. When we got up to leave after she'd insisted we stay even longer, it was as if we were abandoning her.

"Don't leave so soon."

It was very late, almost dawn. She laughed as if to excuse herself.

"I hate being alone. I like the warmth of others. That's why I want to work all the time. Fortunately. . . ."

She pointed again at the photographs on the wall.

"Fortunately I have all this to reassure me. I know I'm alive when I see myself."

Emptiness in one's self, the absence of spirit like a tree that is hollow, drives people in search of fame, the éclat of honors, the rumors of notoriety. But these are never enough to muffle the enormous grumbling of our interior void.

We attempt to cover it by an ever wider fame, more honors, an even noisier notoriety. But in one's self the void grows accordingly.

And sooner or later a day comes, which may be any time, may be at the beginning of the second half of life or in old age, when the void prevails: it is there like an abyss. Which fame, notoriety and amibition have never been able to fill, which on the contrary they have deepened day by day.

We left for France without seeing Jane again. When Nicole was born in New York, where we'd returned after buying Barons to make preparations for moving to what would be our fortress, Dina telephoned her. I was sitting watching Dina, imagining in her silences the excessive talkativeness of Jane, her laughter. Dina hung up with a fatigued air.

"Jane's not doing too well, I'm afraid," she said.

I was astonished. I had heard her exclamations, her bursts of laughter.

"She's doing too well," Dina continued. "Always the same, roles, fame, success. She's sending us two seats for tomorrow night to see her dance. If you'd like to. . . ."

Jane seemed to be happy in this spectacle which evoked the days of the French can-can. We waited for her after the show. She came in, tired, her features drawn, voice too high—a face like a mask. She embraced Dina.

"You see, everything's going well. I've arrived. They've promised me the lead role in the next play. The star, Dina, the star."

"And Harold?"

"What Harold?"

She laughed as always, and excused herself. She couldn't have dinner with us. I was glad.

A few years later, I happened to read in the European edition of the *New York Herald Tribune* that Jane had committed suicide. Like so many show people before her.

The pursuit of these mirages, of fame and notoriety, the attempt to reach the bottom of abysses that have no bottom. The futile hope that the image that others make of you will cease trembling like a reflection in flowing water, that it will finally swim into focus–all this can only lead to an ever more frantic search for more fame, more notoriety.

Unless you suddenly realize that this search will never end, that what it lacks will always be more than what it has.

It can break a man. For he has been emptied of himself.

That evening, after putting the children to bed, Dina and I sat up late by the fire. It was raining. Gusts of wind blew it against the bay windows. Two or three times, as it often did during storms, the electricity went off. As I got up to connect the circuit-breaker, Dina held me back.

"Leave it," she said.

The lively fire lit up the room with its golden glow.

"Why?" Dina asked me. "Why Jane?"

But it was less a question to me than something she was asking herself.

"She had succeeded in what she wanted to do. . . ."

"Succeeded?"

Success? What does that mean?

I had known men of all sorts, in extreme circumstances.

Success for some, like those Polish peasants who robbed me of money that could have saved my life, meant the accumulation of gold, silver, wealth. For the storm troopers who searched the mouths of gassed victims for their gold fillings, it was also gold, that yellow metal that made their eyes gleam. And in New York I had seen the same trembling flame in so many men's eyes. Success, to be rich. That is what the word meant. And perhaps for a few days, a few months, when my ventures began to yield their profit like a ripe fruit its juice, that is the meaning that I myself assigned the word. But this dollar chase soon appeared to me as futile, insufficient. What could I do with this money if I remained alone? A day would come when I was a millionaire. When I had enough to eat and live on, when I had succeeded—this money permitted me to do—in loosening the vice of necessity, what more did these dollars bring me?

Success is not that flight which disguises itself as a pursuit of wealth.

It was not success to become one of those self-satisfied men who lived for their businesses and talked only of money.

I had had friends—but were they really friends?—whom I sometimes got together with on weekends for a game of cards or an outing. Douglas was our guide. He knew the fashionable cafes, the French or Italian restaurants in New York. He showed us his latest model car, made us share in

the decorating of his apartment which he changed
every six months. And we had to admire his latest liaisons.
His girls were almost too beautiful. And he always talked
business. As if his only outlet was the recital of his gains by
telling us his expenses.

"Not bad is it, Martin, even you're surprised. I'm quin-
tupling my outlay."

He offered us champagne. He offered himself a new
woman. When I went into the antiques business, Douglas
attracted and fascinated me as a model. And that was why
he liked me: I was one of those admirers he needed for his
profits and expenses to acquire meaning. When I knew him
better I realized the void that underlay this showy front and
efficient restlessness.

> *To live, to realize your life, cannot be to reduce it to a*
> *mere desire for possession of things, of money.*
> *Success cannot mean the accumulation of inert matter.*
> *What is it to live thus, but to slowly bury yourself in*
> *possessions?*

Light was cast for me on all this when I later met Dina,
who introduced me to men who met not to play cards or talk
business, but to share their ideas or the pleasure of listening together to a symphony.

I listened to Karl, a German emigrant with an enthusiasm undimmed by time who lived in harmony with
the world's events. It seemed that his personal life encom-

passed Berlin, Moscow, the Middle East and the Korean front. That the world's demographic growth, a discovery of prehistoric remains that dated further back in time than the appearance of man on earth, were his private affairs.

To succeed is to live a multiple life, expanded to the dimensions of the world. To succeed is to participate at least in spirit in the collective destiny of man.

I understood this little by little. But what I felt when I listened to Douglas and my then friends was that they mutilated life. I knew how precious it was. I knew from having fought, from having seen so many of my brothers die in Warsaw and Treblinka, that one must respect it. And if I had lived only to amass dollars, to change the decor of my apartment or the model of my car, then those I'd loved would have been right to ask me from the depths of death's exile:

"Is this why you have saved your life?"

I listened to Douglas, I observed my friends. They had in their hands an inestimable good, life. What were they doing with it? Sometimes I said to myself that they were less than the ants I liked to study when my father took me into the forest before the war. In their feverish activities they at least were building for the anthill, were parts of a whole. I remembered their laborious columns, persistently transporting and reconstructing; and then I saw us, myself, Douglas, Jimmy and a few others, each of us locked in our egotistic lives, interested only in ourselves, in our little successes and pleasures. A well-managed affair, an unexpected windfall.

Was this life? And if it was, what an abyss. Why live?

Like myself, Douglas and my friends, the girls they went around with, and later Jane, were confusedly aware that their lives were turning in a void. On certain evenings, Douglas accompanied me back to my place. Because he liked me and because he knew that he could talk to me without being taken advantage of, he asked me questions in a low, suddenly tired voice.

"Martin, tell me, why are we running around this way? You with your trips, Berlin, Paris, me with this frantic activity all week—what's it for? Don't you think it's slightly crazy?"

I was standing in the door. He kept my hand in his. Then he shook his head and mumbled some indistinct phrases.

"What do I have this evening? I can't stop even for one evening."

For Douglas, work, affairs, money, all these were his drugs. For Jane, the drug was notoriety.

And later these drugs were no longer enough. Other drugs were tried. Absences, nervous depressions which were flights from the void of their lives.

When the emptiness in our lives is too deep, when our
life passes in grasping possession of objects that melt
away from us like ice, when we try to hold on to a
handful of water, when we discover that possession is
an ephemeral joy and one must always possess more,
then we fall into the abyss of depression. It is the
malady of a life with no goal worthy of life. It is our
being's protest against the squandering of our life, its
mutilation and diminishment.

I discovered this in my talks with Karl, in questioning
him, in remembering what my life had been in the ghetto.

A life reduced to itself is not a life. It is an amputation
of life. And it leads only to the abysses of solitude and
an awareness of failure.

In New York, I had set up a flourishing business. I
traveled around Europe visiting antique dealers. I was free,
in danger neither of prison nor death. I was rich. And yet I
was empty.

With fear and astonishment, I meditated on what I had
been, the days in the ghetto when I had smuggled the
wheat of survival into my starving city. I no longer felt that
strength in my hands, that joy of seizing the sacks of grain
which I had once known. The contraband goods that I
handed out to the people who crowded around me in the
streets of the ghetto.

Why this nostalgic memory of a terrible period which I had nonetheless lived with passion?

I knew the answer. I found it during one of my airplane flights which took me in the same week to London, Paris, Berlin. I was empty because I was alone, I worked for myself alone, for my bank account, my future. Of course in the ghetto I'd also worked for myself. But I knew that in my way I was giving lifeblood to my people. That was why I'd lived passionately and why, in New York, I no longer found that passion of action except in memory. It was a true answer. But within myself there was an uncertainty as to the future, a mounting dissatisfaction despite my success.

Fortunately, I had retained a goal which was for myself but also outside myself: to found a family, a fortress of life. It was that for which I worked, for which I acted and lived. Fortunately, I met Dina and my life found its direction. But the others, who remained closed in themselves?

> *In devoting ourselves to our own interests, in conforming to the rule of this time that one act primarily for one's self, we think we are working in our own favor. We think we are amassing goods. In reality, we are casting them into a void.*
>
> *The man who opens himself to others enriches his life.*
>
> *For the richness of a life is enthusiasm and joy. And these come only with transcendence of self. The man who seeks to possess only for himself inhabits a desert, he buries himself under his goods.*

Those who go toward others, who live with others, find the oasis.

Later, in the course of evenings we spent with Karl and Dina's friends, when I had finally found peace, when I heard men speak as men—of men and not of things—I would often talk, with Karl first whose gray eyes and serene old age I loved, of the void which I had felt open in me and seen open in others. I told Karl that I had come to feel nostalgia for the solidarity of the ghetto. At least in the midst of barbarism I knew I was among brothers. Then I told him about the tenacious ants who worked for their ant nation. Karl laughed.

"You want to build the anthill again? Your dream is to disappear into a group, to be part of it, whereas I have simply to look at you to know that you are an individualist, a solitary."

I denied this and yet I knew that what he said was true.

"But it is only natural," Karl said. "You are right to want to. The void does exist. Only it is not the world of the ants that we must recreate. It is the world of men which has never seen the light. We must rediscover in ourselves that solidarity which, for example, unites the members of a tribe. That solidarity, Martin, yes, but retain the individuality which is our riches."

I went back with Dina. New York was no longer a disquieting city in which muggers lay in wait for passersby. Yet we still were aware, Dina and I, of the city's violence,

its brutal grandeur. The streets dwarfed by towering buildings, the derelicts, the black ghettos. I was able to compare
it with the small cities of Europe, whose dimensions remained human. One night, we saw young blacks hurl
stones through windows of stores out in Brooklyn. Then
they fled as the howling sirens of the police arrived.

"I want us to leave the city," Dina said. "And yet I love
it."

I loved it also. But it was harsh. Indifferent to a man's
plight, this derelict, this old Negro. Years later, I was to find
in front of my hotel in Paris another derelict, also abandoned in the indifference of a great city. Perhaps it was the
city that forced men to be these mad wheels that whirled
incessantly in febrile activity. Money, fame, more money.

The city where trees died, their roots stifling under the
cement.

*The city, cities that are too large, like diseased excres-
cences, enormous tumors.*

There rootless men are ignorant of each others' lives.

*And the cities grow endlessly; they are deepening abys-
ses in which brotherly custom is lost. The long looks,
the smiles.*

*These cities in which men jostle each other like grains of
sand, where they are nothing, these cities where one
must recreate peace, joy, the ties of acquaintance and
affection between men.*

I also learned this for myself, later. When, after living ten years with Dina and my children in our isolated country house, I returned to Paris—grown tenfold, its frenzy, its traffic jams. I remember a night in November. It was raining hard, I'd come in from the airport at Orly and my taxi was wedged in an inextricable jam. In front of us, a man left his car and began shouting and pounding on the door of the car ahead of him. Unable to open it, he abused the driver and kicked at the car.

"As if being stuck wasn't enough," my driver said. "They have to fight too."

Violence: the malady of the city too big for itself.
Violence, the wild explosion of man's revolt against his empty and absurd life.
Violence which blames others, which blames itself. Destruction and self-destruction, violence which chooses the other as its victim, its target, sometimes because of its skin color, sometimes randomly. Violence, the drug of our time.
Violence like an erring energy, a headlong torrent, a destroying flood that must be dammed.

Perhaps because I had become hypersensitive since my tragedy, because my wounds were still raw, I felt personally attacked by violence. I could not indifferently observe the derelict squatting in the gutter, the men who insulted each other in the street, the photographs of children muti-

lated in the Asian war. I could not but be pained by young
people in rags whose gleaming eyes bespoke their drug-
craving. I saw them cross the street without a glance at the
traffic. They possessed an inestimable good, youth, and yet
they seemed to already have lost the gift of enthusiasm. I
looked at them and I suffered for them, in myself. One
night, returning to my hotel, I felt a pang of depression at
the idea of being alone and went to one of the noisy, color-
ful cafes in the Latin Quarter. At the next table, a young
man was listlessly thumbing through an issue of *Time*.
Wearing a furred leather jacket, dirty, he seemed cold. I
hesitated, then spoke to him in English.

"No good? You're studying in Europe?"

He took a long time answering me. Hardly raising his
head, he informed me that he was in fact studying architecture and urbanism. He was visiting the European capitals.

"But, you know, architecture today . . . so I'm living like
this."

I tried to make him talk about himself. Little by little he
came alive. He asked questions angrily.

"Architecture? Who are they building for? Money, that's
what runs everything. Architecture? Even in Paris there are
skyscrapers like in New York or Chicago, look. . . ."

On the Boulevard St. Michel cars backed up, luminous
carcasses in a sort of long, immobile caterpillar.

"That's urbanism today. People are wiped out. All these
poor jerks who spend three hours a day in their cars. I have
a room in Saint-Cloud. I see them choking to death in the
tunnel in their little boxes on wheels."

"Exactly," I said. "Since you're an urbanist, you'll have to form a new conception of the city."

"You're naïve. The city is this. It can't be anything else. It can't be changed. Done for. I get out from under as I can, in my way."

Later he asked me for some money, which I gave him. Perhaps for drugs or alcohol. But what could I do? Refuse him? I tried to convince him, to give him courage by what I said. I don't think I succeeded. I stayed in the cafe until I was told they were closing. I saw other young faces, also jaded. I watched them sagging against the counter. Nearly all of them were lost for a life worthy of the name. Who had thrown them into these abysses of despair?

Our cities which obliterate men. Our harsh societies which implacably reject the weak. Our secret laws by which money and profit rule.

Our mores which exalt violence or escape from the real into the illusions of drug or alcohol.

The inequities which make the rich and strong richer and stronger, the weak and poor weaker and poorer.

Our society too often like a jungle, a concentration camp without brotherhood among its inmates, who pursue their lives indifferent to each other.

All this leads to these lost lives, abandoned or caught in mortal impasses.

I experienced again my impressions of the time in New York when, as a door-to-door salesman, I went through the

big apartment buildings in the Bronx. I discovered then
those somber apartments, those lives shut in a cell of the
hive, bound to dull jobs. Menaced by all the ills that plague
man and by the ills of societies, unemployment, fear, anguish.

Was it to live this life that men were men? I could only
live it with the hope that one day another would come.

> *The world would be other. Man rid of the chains of
> inequality, the weight of a social organization which
> crushes him.*
> *Man finally freed from his shackles.*
> *Man finally enabled to confront his problems, his true
> questions, his perduring and noble anguishes. Happi-
> ness, the why and how of his life, the interrogation of
> death.*
> *But a man who is hungry, a man who is afraid, cannot
> think freely of these things. He gropes like a blind
> man.*

I relived the war, the ghetto. I observed the anarchic
traffic of the cities, the gray crowds, the young disqualified
from living. The derelicts, beggars, our world without real
justice. I observed the joyless faces of the great city.

> *Yes, we are still living in the abyss.*
> *Yes, man is still in his prehistory.*
> *He must emerge from it.*

188

Of course for this it would be necessary to change some of our laws. That from above, those who have power modify their style of government, their world-view. That the squandering of the rich come to an end.

For there are billions of men who are hungry. And their numbers are increasing daily.
Today, we are three and a half billion.
Tomorrow-in less than thirty years-we will be more than seven billion. Then the inequalities between men, the superabundance for some, poverty for the majority, will not merely be an insult to the dignity of man, whatever the color of his skin. Then inequality will be a menace to all men. We have our backs to an abyss. To refuse to see it will not make it disappear.
To avoid toppling into it we must face it-and then go away from it. Justice and equality must be established. For reasons of morality and because justice and equality are more and more the safest ways.
But for humanity to advance along these new roads, it is not enough for a few men to decide on it. All men, and firstly those who are no longer hungry, must understand its necessity.
Because the thought and will of men are an immense force.

I remember our insurrection in the ghetto. We were nothing. We had only a few weapons. But we had the will to fight, we wanted to hold out for a few hours at least. And we fought for weeks. If we had risen during the first months of our servitude and humiliation, when we numbered 500,000, who could have defeated us?

But the shackles were not merely those on our feet. The will and spirit in too many of us had been subjugated. The executioners skillfully played with our weaknesses. Held out false hopes. Later when, having escaped from Treblinka, I tried to explain to those who were still free, unaware of the inferno that awaited them, I was not believed. My listeners were invariably incredulous. I was treated as a fool.

The fool is not he who states the problem that exists, the disease that is spreading but that still may be healed. The fool is he who closes his eyes, who covers his head, who refuses to hear. For a day will come when the problem is there, the cancer present, and there will be no time.

Since I created my foundation for the protection of nature, met scientists and received information on the problems of our time which until then I had not known, I discovered that, as in the ghetto, most men—and myself until recently—refused to see. Therefore men did not act, and allowed themselves to be pushed by circumstances to the brink of the abyss.

Myself, I knew now. As I had after Treblinka.

Man is at a crossing of the ways. Before him, for the first time, a future whose features he can envision if he does nothing: each year men increasing by millions, soon to be billions on this earth, and the disorder of a production that destroys soil, water and even the sky. At the end of this road await violence, disorder and hunger.

But there is another road.

That of wishing to change. To utilize the power of man for himself and not against himself.

And for that there is one force: the knowledge of man, of each man who, feeling himself concerned, directly threatened, will choose the other way. That way leads to the peaceful organization of the world.

I am no more than the voice of a man who has known the barbarism of war, who has seen men become beasts. I am no more than the voice of a witness, a man who has lost all that was dear to him. By the absurd fire that raged through an unprotected forest.

I am nothing more than the voice of a man who knows that it is possible to preserve man and his future.

In the summer that followed my tragedy I made an appeal to men of good will to defend what remained of the forest from new conflagrations.

I was at les Barons and young people came to me, the young who are nonetheless said to care only about themselves.

"We are with you," they told me. One of them, a tall stooping young man, badly dressed and unshaven, filled his knapsack with the Foundation's brochures.

"I'm going to distribute these," he said.

He gave me a wink.

"If we do nothing, they'll ruin everything. They have to know, have to understand. We'll talk to them."

All that summer, on the Côte d 'Azur visited by millions of tourists, he and other young people worked gratis for the Foundation. And that year the number of forest fires decreased.

I remember the skeptical journalist who heard me give the results achieved by the Foundation.

"The climate helped you this summer, just the same," he repeated.

I pretended not to hear him, but when he began again I lost my temper.

"The climate is nothing," I shouted. "Don't you know yet that the weather also depends on man?"

It was an excessive reaction, and yet true.

The weather would change if the forests were destroyed. North of Tanneron, before the fire, we had the sky of the Midi. Now, when the trees were no more than dead trunks, fog clung to the ground and the sun was veiled. Now, the wind blew in gusts and days of torrid heat succeeded freezing nights.

But we were able to modify this weather. One day in spring, each of the schoolchildren of Tanneron went out with a young tree in their hands. They climbed the rocky slopes, dug and planted the trees of spring. The weather, one day soon because men wished for it, would be as it had been before the fire.

I remembered for a long time the eyes and face of that child who, with awkward hands, set his tree in the earth.

Man, if he wishes, can fill in the abysses that lie along his way.

He can always, by a dead tree, plant a tree of life.

But he must wish to. He must dare to face the danger and denounce it.

He must not resign himself to the madness of acceptance.

Then his future will be green, the weather clement.

DESTINY

This evening I was alone in the great empty room at Barons. Through the bay window I saw the distant sea. Suddenly I saw only the iron bars Dina had had fastened across the window to prevent the entry of prowlers into our isolated house. It seemed to me that these bars shut in my life. I remembered that day when Max Gallo showed me the verse from the Old Testament he'd chosen for the beginning of his preface. "Your life, Martin," he said, "truly reminds me of Job whom God, to try him, stripped of everything." The verse described Job given over to Satan.

This evening, I reread the quotation. I asked myself whether there wasn't a destiny which had chosen since birth to obliterate me. If I wasn't the victim of forces within myself or over me that imprisoned me. Like these bars.

A destiny, my destiny which, when I sought peace, when I thought I had found it, had led me to live here so as to become the victim of a forest fire, of death, of a war.

Is fate a reality?

*Are we held in a hand that, as it wills, spares or muti-
lates us?*
*In us, or outside us, from the day of our birth, is the
road we must travel already laid down?*
Must one believe in destiny?

This evening, perhaps because the winter night fell
quickly, because my solitude oppressed me, I was not able
to answer the question. I let my own questions, images and
memories arise in me. The other day a friend told me the
story of those curious fowl, the "mutton birds," who, when
their parents have abandoned them in the nest, set out on a
flight of some 15,000 miles over the Pacific before returning
to the nests.

A flight which all mutton birds have accomplished since
time immemorial and apparently without motive. If not at
the summons of some imperious will. Their destiny, inscribed in their being, which compells them to this journey
and guides them on it.

Is our life similarly guided?
*Are we free in our choices, or are we driven toward our
fate blindfolded, capable of nothing?*

These questions have haunted me, I have always kept
them in mind.

And who does not question himself?

One evening, when we visited a couple of friends, we

198

found only Maria in. Usually she took care of their children.

"They all went out," she said with a laugh. "To the open air movie. They wanted to take me with them but I refused. Somehow or other I want to be alone."

Late that night we had a phone call. A robber had gotten into the villa and attacked Maria. We went to see her the next day. She was covered with bruises but remained calm, shaking her head, passive.

"It was fate," she said. "There was nothing I could have done. It was in the cards. You know, if I'd gone with them to the movies something else would have happened, an accident. I know. That night was marked. One cannot escape one's fate."

This evening, I thought of Maria.

My most terrible thoughts recurred to me, those which leave me no chance, which tell my history like something in stone: I survive my family in Treblinka, I escape the destruction of the ghetto, I make my fortune, I encounter love, Dina, we finally have children, and all to have it end in fire and their death?

Am I a marked man? Prisoner of a mysterious destiny?

I went out and walked along the road that for so long had been a pathway of joy. The fresh air did me good. Restored my reason.

What is destiny?

A name that man gives to events, a chain he makes to connect their diverse facts?

*A chain that shackles him if he accepts it. But he must
always wish to break it.*
*And if it is heavy, if it seems to resist, the effort to break
it is the true meaning of man's life.*

Destiny?

I had seen so many men abase themselves before this
word, kneel to await its verdict. Thousands in the ghetto
who day after day gave themselves up to the sword of their
destiny. And who can condemn them? They are my dead
brothers.

Myself, I seized the first chance. I refused to believe in
the destiny that made me one of the humiliated, vanquished, a slave, a corpse. I fled, I fought, I survived. When
after my tragedy, the death of my loved ones, the people of
Tanneron learned that previously I'd escaped death in the
ghetto and Treblinka, they always said—and one of them,
an old peasant with wrinkled skin, told me:

"Martin Gray is a man destined not to die, a man who
escapes everything. It's his destiny. That's how it is."

No, that's not how it is.

When I considered those years of violence and barbarism, when I looked at my hands still marked by torture,
when lifting my arms I felt the pain in my shoulders, physical memory of the cells of Pawiak prison in Warsaw, where
I was hung by the wrists and beaten, I knew that destiny
makes itself.

Man has two roads always before him.
And he must choose between them.
Two roads before his eyes, two destinies.
And at each step there is a new crossing.
Two roads, two possible destinies.
And he will travel so until the last second of his life.

I know that later, to others, it often all seems simple.
When I recounted my various escapes to Max Gallo as he
took them down in his notebook, I would often stop, irritated that he did not stop me.

"You understand," I asked him, "you know that I could
easily have stayed behind with the others? You must make
the readers understand this. I am not a hero, Max, but I
want the readers to know that nothing is easy. That one
must want it. Do you understand, Max?"

Nothing is ever completely settled. There is never a
single road, a single destiny.
We must know that we can, that we should choose.
But we must want to choose. To believe that it is possi-
ble.
That we build our destiny with our own hands.
That it is always an open road.
That as long as there is a breath of life there is the hope
of choice and change. Of one's self and the world.

I knew of so many examples that proved that our destiny

was not like that of migratory birds, inscribed in our hearts
and minds.

> *Man is not merely an assemblage of wheels, an amassing
> of materials. He is firstly a decision, and each posses-
> ses in himself, if he wishes it, if he knows it, the possi-
> bility of constructing, of producing something with
> his wheels and materials.*
> *For each man is unique. And each man must wish to be
> unique even if he knows his solidarity with others.*

When I was working in New York I lived for a while in a
southern suburb. Nearby in a big white house lived a couple I rarely saw. But often when I came back late I would
hear sinister howlings, a human voice that had never
achieved speech. I learned later that it was their son, a
retarded child who occasionally suffered fits of rage. I was
thinking of having a family and children, and for several
days I retained the horrifying image of the fate that had
befallen this couple. One night I found myself alone in the
road with a man still young, with a noble face and long
blond hair combed straight back from his forehead.

"Sir, I believe you live in the house next door. . . . ," he
began. Then when we'd arrived in front of his house:

"I ask you, sir, please. . . ."

I hesitated. It is always difficult to confront the unjustest
misery, that which strikes children.

"I beg you,"· he repeated.

I followed him inside. His wife had gentle eyes and a relaxed smile.

"I'm happy to meet you," she told me.

We talked for a few minutes, and then they said at almost the same time:

"It would give us pleasure if you saw Frank, our son, and what he does."

I could only accept.

Seated on the floor in a large room was an adolescent with bowed head and twitching face, a jutting chin and an upper lip already downed with black hair. When he saw us he gave a sort of groan and shook his head several times.

"He's happy to see you," his father said.

I was paralyzed. Horrified. And yet it was a familiar horror. But here, this mutilated child, the fate of this couple.

"Look," the father said to me.

It was then that I saw the walls were covered with paintings. Gay paintings in which bright colors dominated, the gold of a joyous sun, blue and red. I saw that Frank had been painting with jerky gestures when we'd come in, that on the canvas placed on the floor a sort of huge radiant flower was being born.

"Frank has done all this," the mother told me. "It's beautiful. When he paints, he becomes calm. For me, these flowers are his soul."

Fate.
Not to bow one's head before what is called fate.
To learn from the event which befalls us a strength for
ourselves and for others.
Not to submit to what has apparently destroyed us.
But, on the contrary, to lift with both hands this weight
that is upon us, to hold it at arm's length. To wish to
do so.
To want to put aside this heavy weight so as to finally
see the sky. And each can see his sky.

Frank's parents had found painting for him. They had
not given in to the situation but had fought it hand to hand.
And they had won. I also remembered the writer Max Gallo
told me about, a man stricken with polio when he was
barely thirty. Who had known how to create a life for himself, despite his paralysis. To write, to express himself, to
realize that a great work had been his means of overcoming
his fate and making another for himself.

At each moment, the cards are changing in the game of
life. Yesterday illness, today health. Today happiness
and peace, tomorrow unhappiness and despair.
But we are always able to build with what has been
given us.
As long as a man is alive he can always rebuild, even
with ruins.

Only, it is easier when the materials are sound.

I realized this for myself so often in my life: the lack of sleep, fatigue, the wear and tear of the body are what sap the will. They are what enslaves us.

Dina and I had understood this. We had given up wine, and even meat. Each can choose his way. But I know that one has to reckon with one's body.

It is a man's duty not to squander his strength. Not to exhaust his body through excess.
For a man is a whole.
Thought is not clear, will is not unshakeable when body tone is dull. Thought is like water.
It can be troubled, made muddy if the body itself is troubled and full of mud.

I tried to explain this to Jacques M. who worked with me at the Foundation. He laughed at what he ironically called my "alimentary manias." We often had to invite journalists to lunch. Each time I had to explain, almost excuse myself so as not to start with a whiskey, followed by Bordeaux wine. I watched the others drink more than they should. They took the restaurant menu in their hands with a passion that struck me as curious. What I grudged them was not their preference for this or that entree. It was that they ate too much. After the meal, Jacques was in a torpor. He would order another cup of coffee. He was caught in the vicious circle of overeating, alcohol and the abuse of stimulants. All this seemed to me a form of escapism.

And I had known it myself during my first years in New York, when I experienced the harshness of solitude. I drank then. Restaurants at that time were temples of pleasure for me. To eat was a way of proving that the world belonged to me. Enveloped in the cold of solitude, the passing warmth afforded by alcohol and richly prepared food allowed me for a moment to forget my situation.

I would grow euphoric. But then would come the consequences: my thought clouded, my energy diminished and a sensation of loneliness ever more difficult to bear.

That is why I changed, ate less. Discovered the joy of simple dishes. Of clear water. Of a light body.

> *A man, if he does not wish for his life to slip between his fingers before he is aware of it, must know how to control his appetites. Sometimes to limit them.*
> *He must know that his health is capital which he must not squander.*
> *It is this capital that makes him rich.*
> *If he wishes to conserve it, he must choose moderation and simplicity.*
> *He must refuse the easy, beckoning slope of pleasures.*
> *He must reject these pleasures, real but in the end secondary, which may if he seeks them too often prevent him from achieving higher, more durable joys.*
> *Here also one must choose.*

To know which is best: the transient warmth of alcohol
or the cool, clear water of life.

I looked at Jacques. He drank slowly, and I could read in his gestures the pleasure this red, velvety wine afforded him. A few years ago, he had told me, he'd been the victim of an ulcer. One day, leaving the office, brutal stomach pains had bent him double. Perforated ulcer. Immediate operation.

"Since then, no trouble," he told me. "I can eat and drink as before. Martin, you will never know what it means, this cheese with a glass of red wine." I did know. I knew everything about wine and other drinks. Yet I had given them up and felt no desire for them. For Jacques, they were indispensable. Despite the risks he was taking with his health and risks I tried to explain to him. Why did he keep doing it? Was it really a need? Of the same kind that forced young addicts to search endlessly for one more dose, to waste their lives in a brief career of illusory joys? But was it really a question of the body? In fact it concerned their spirit, the self, character.

When a man lacks goals that transcend him, when he
has lost the hope of a life to his measure, when he has
given up trying to reach the peak and lives from day
to day, not knowing where he is going: then he flees
down these shabby streets of mediocre pleasures.

*And he may lose himself in them. Compromise his
health. And by just so much weaken his courage, di-
minish his thought, sink himself deeper in his slough.*

It was Dina who gave me the strength to choose the true
joys. Which are not those of alcohol, nor of eating, nor of any
drug. With her, I no longer needed these mediocre pleasures. I had found my harbor, my peace. I had cast anchor. I
had my children before me. I watched them run, grow, I
heard them play the piano. I wanted to live long so as to
protect them, to see them as they blossomed. I wanted to
see what kind of adults they would become. I had achieved
happiness. I no longer needed alcohol. A juicy fruit was
enough for me: my joy, their joy, my hope were my al-
cohols.

No doubt it was this that Jacques lacked. He was divorced and lived alone. He was not interested much in
others. He had come to the Foundation because he'd
needed a job rather than to devote himself to a cause. He
was not happy.

*For a man to achieve plenitude, to be truly a man, he
must create a world in which he is the center.
This can be a work: the painting of an artist, the piece of
a cabinetmaker, the field of a peasant, the page of a
writer.
It can be a family.
For man has a need to become the strong column of a
temple he has built and sustains.*

208

Now, I am once more alone. But there are the letters I have received by the thousands. There is this book I have written which will speak to others. In my solitude I have once more become an erect column. My life has a direction in the fraternity of others.

For cold reason is not enough for a man.
It is merely the soil that must have water to germinate.
The water is love, is others, is the hope and the belief
    that tomorrow, in each man and first of all one's self,
    the fresh and the beautiful will have sprung up.
The certainty that man will be able to live in peace and
    joy, with himself and others.
And if suffering comes, and it will come since death will
    always be there, the hope that man will take this suf-
    fering into his hands and make it a fruit. To derive
    from it the certainty that one must live a higher, bet-
    ter life. In this fragile miracle which is life.

I have come through. I am on my way. The fog has lifted and the immense night observes me.

I have the right to march, head high, my face turned to that somber sky.

I have the right to say that I have tried to live like a man.

This day I have finished *A Book of Life.*

I would like to hold it out to others as I once held out my hand to my children. Not because I imagine myself to be a wise man.

But I have the right to speak. Mine is a humble superior-

ity, that of my suffering. That of my voice, when it speaks.
When it says:

> *That life is indestructible. Despite death.*
> *That hope is a fresh wind that must blow away despair.*
> *That another is a friend before he is an enemy.*
> *That we must live lives charged with love and hope.*
> *That we must bring together in ourselves those diverse*
> *aspects which constitute our personality.*
> *That one must believe in noble words: fraternity, duty,*
> *respect for men.*

When my voice rises and repeats:

> *That one must never despair of one's self and the world.*
> *That the strengths in us, which can raise us up, are im-*
> *mense. That our will holds an unsuspected power.*
> *That we can always, if we wish to, reconstruct our lives.*

When my voice goes on:

> *That we must speak of love and not the words of stormy*
> *disorder.*
> *But that we must know how to risk all to defend a truth,*
> *a principle of brotherhood. And that one must be wil-*
> *ling occasionally to fight one's self and others as well*
> *who allow the demons of barbarism to rise up in*
> *themselves.*

When my voice calls out:

That the royal destiny of man and his torment is to begin again, to carry farther this flame of his hope, despite death which comes like a sea to rub out his footprints in the sand, and to begin again as he must, to banish fear and begin once again.

When I shout:

That life begins today and every day, and that it is hope.

You must believe me. I have lived what I tell you.

AUTHOR'S NOTE

I have written this book in order to understand life, my own life, and I have written it for you, hoping to be of use.

If, as I hope, it has been able to help you, to give the beginnings of answers to questions every man asks himself, then I ask you—but doubtless you have already understood—to tell others of this book, who like myself and like you have need of a friendly voice that speaks to them.

If you wish, write me:

Martin Gray
Domaine les Barons
Tanneron, 83141, France

I will be happy to continue with you the dialogue begun in *For Those I Loved* and continued here in *A Book of Life*.